# Above the Clearwater

*Living on Stolen Land*

# Above the Clearwater

## Living on Stolen Land

*Bette Lynch Husted*

**Oregon State University Press**
Corvallis

The paper in this book meets the guidelines for permanence and durability of the Committee on Production Guidelines for Book Longevity of the Council on Library Resources and the minimum requirements of the American National Standard for Permanence of Paper for Printed Library Materials Z39.48-1984.

**Library of Congress Cataloging-in-Publication Data**
Husted, Bette Lynch.
  Above the Clearwater : living on stolen land / Bette Lynch Husted.—1st ed.
    p. cm.
  ISBN 0-87071-007-9 (alk. paper)
  1. Clearwater River Valley (Idaho)—History. 2. Frontier and pioneer life—Idaho—Clearwater River Valley. 3. Pioneers—Idaho—Clearwater River Valley—History. 4. Nez Perce Indians—Land tenure—Idaho—Clearwater River Valley—History.
  5. Clearwater River Valley (Idaho)—Race relations. 6. Husted, Bette Lynch. 7. Lynch family. 8. Pioneers—Idaho—Clearwater River Valley—Biography. 9. Clearwater River Valley (Idaho)—Biography.
  I. Title.
  F752.C62 H87 2004
  979.6'85—dc22
                              2003019389

**Oregon State University Press**
101 Waldo Hall
Corvallis OR 97331-6407
541-737-3166 • fax 541-737-3170
http://oregonstate.edu/dept/press

OREGON STATE
UNIVERSITY

# Contents

# Acknowledgments

Several essays or parts of essays were first published in these journals or anthologies:

"Water Stories," in *Northern Lights*, Volume XIII, Number 4, Fall 1998

"Following the Deer," in *Northwest Review*, volume 37, Number 3, 1999

Parts of "On Water and On Land," as "Coyote's Friend Fox," in *Natural Bridge*, Number 4, Fall 2000

"Guns," in *Talking River Review*, Winter 2002

"Salmon Run," in *Best Essays NW: Perspectives from Oregon Quarterly*. Editors Guy Maynard and Kathleen Holt. Eugene: University of Oregon Press, 2003

Thanks to Fishtrap Writing Workshops and Fishtrap director Rich Wandschneider, and to The Flight of the Mind Writing Workshops for Women and its founders Judith Barrington and Ruth Gundle, and the teachers I met in these workshops who have shown me how to listen to the stories, especially Judith, Naomi Nye, Alex Kuo, Rosellen Brown, Ursula Le Guin, Lucille Clifton, and Grace Paley.

Thanks also to Judith Barrington and Ruth Gundle and the Soapstone Board and all the volunteers who make the Soapstone Writing Retreat for Women possible, to Judith and Ruth for ongoing encouragement and invaluable assistance; to Wallowa County librarian Claudia Jones; to Caroline Le Guin, Paul Williams, and Shelley Davidow for reading and writing; and to editor Mary Elizabeth Braun, who understood.

And thank you to the Indian people who have tried to teach me, Starla and Lucinda and Raymond and Cecelia and so many others.

Deep thanks to all my family, and for my family—especially my mother Irene, whose lifelong blessings made writing possible; Dean, whose love and support led to this book; and Josh, who came home.

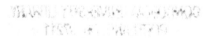

# Looking for Home

# Indians

It was a big fire: everything was burning—the log walls and the windows and the roof, even my mother's arm was on fire, alive with sparks, and my father's heart, roaring like the flames. He pushed a cardboard box out the window and leaped after it just as the ceiling collapsed in an explosion of sparks and the house swallowed itself. Then the shouting stopped, and my father and mother forgot how to speak. They gathered my sister and me into the old truck and drove away into the deep snow. Over my mother's shoulder, out the rearview window, I could see the fire still burning: a circle of orange in an all-white world. My fingers burned too, with the cold, but we had no coats, no blankets. I wanted to go back to the fire. I wanted to go home. No, Mama told me. Everything is gone.

But it wasn't, really. Three weeks after the fire—it was 1947, I was not quite two—we were living in an old rough-board shack at the western edge of the ranch, in the shadow of the big yellow pine. The log house my grandfather had built had become a black pile of ashes that I could find if I climbed on the big bed and looked out the window, but home was still here, all around me. There was the barn and the east field beyond it, and the barnyard trees, and the hills rising up on either side of me. Looking out that window, I knew there was something else out there, too. Something else "home" meant besides the old log house. Indian people. I couldn't see them, but they were there.

When I was older I would notice that every time the horses walked under that big yellow pine tree into the neighbor's pasture, I could hear a hollow echo in the earth below. Dad thought it was a grave. "Indians are buried there," he said. But that was later, when I was old enough to watch my father standing guard at the kitchen window or at the corner of the back fence and wonder what ghosts stretched their fingers for him in those long pine shadows. The Indians I knew that first winter after the house burned—when we had finally left Grammie's attic bedroom with the coiling black snake ashtray and

3

moved back up the hill into the rough-boarded shack beneath that yellow pine tree—were not under the ground. They were living here with us. But they were always just out of sight, like a smoky shadow behind me that I couldn't quite turn around quickly enough to catch.

After the snow left, home was green. There was bright grass taller than my head. Green-needled pines on the hill climbed up behind the house and dark green firs rimmed the east field. Above us a blue cup had been set upside down on this circle called the world. With darkness came stars and the music of coyotes. When it was light again there were lamb's tongues and clover and hummingbirds and yellow jackets, and the smell of horses. And everywhere—in the sun blazing up from the east field every morning, in the pieces of golden pine puzzle bark that became our toys now, in the blue mountains across the canyon every evening—I knew there were Indians. I could feel them in the spring runoff creek, hear them in the wind when the pines up on the hill talked in one voice.

I missed them.

Now, of course, a voice in my head makes me want to deny all this. A child's imagination, that's all. But it was my first truth. It shapes how I see the world. At a level too deep to dismiss, I *know* it.

We lived at the end of the road, and we had only one book: *Grimm's Fairy Tales*. If the battery for the radio was strong enough, we listened to Jack Benny or Fibber Magee and Molly in the lamplight. Dad told stories about the tepee ring on the spot where he had built his log cabin, just a few yards away from our little house beneath the pine, and sometimes, when I was happy and silly and not really in trouble, he would say, "I'm going to give you back to the Indians."

Yes, Indians had lived here, Mama told me. But now they were gone. When we came to live here—my grandparents and their parents too—the Indians had moved away. Up the river, she said. Her voice sounded sad. We could see the river at the bottom of the canyon when we drove down the steep grade to visit Grammie's house in town, and I wondered where "up the river" was, and how I could get there. "There's an Indian in the river," Mama said. "See? It looks like an Indian man's head. See the nose, and the chin?" But this wasn't what I was looking

4

for. I didn't know a way to tell Mama about the Indians who were still here, beyond the dark tree line of the east field, just out of sight.

One morning I was holding Dad's hand, keeping the clumps of fescue and orchard grass between his knee and me. "Watch for snakes," he said. We were going down the steep slope just below where the old log house had been. "Where was I before?" I asked him. "When you and Mama and Jill were living here without me?"

I looked up. His mouth was moving but he wasn't talking. "Where was I then, Dad? How did I get here?"

Now he was laughing. "You came floating down the river on a raft," he said. Below us the little runoff creek shone in the spring light. "From the Indians!" I said. And I stepped off the hillside, borne into another place. I stood on that raft, my feet feeling for the balance of water and sky; the river spread around me like silver. I could see them on the bank, watching me. Their gaze was pushing me like the current into this journey.

Dad was still laughing, lifting me by one arm around a tuft of root-bound clay. "Take me back," I told him. "I want to go back."

Dad liked to talk about those gloves, smoked buckskin, with the soft gauntlets. An Indian man had stopped to watch him skinning out his buck—this was the year they lived in town, and he was out in the alley behind the little house they'd rented—and after he watched for a long time, the man had asked if he could have the hide. That spring, the man came back with a pair of buckskin gloves. "The best gloves I ever had," Dad said. They were smooth as water and they fit his small, strong hands perfectly. "They were beautiful. But they smelled so smoky I couldn't wear them," he said. "The smoke just ruined them."

I wanted to touch them, pull the gauntlets up over my own wrists. I wanted to hold them up to my face and breathe in, that smoky smell going deep inside me, like the cold well water from the dipper. But they had burned in the fire.

I grew up with the wrong stories. Once I decided to spend the night downtown with my grandmother, and after the others had gone

5

home I told her how I'd found a trail up the hill to a secret place where you could sit right inside a big pine tree. You could hear things. But she said it was dangerous, I shouldn't be going up into those woods, and she told me how once, a long time ago, her father had trapped a grizzly. Dug a big pit and made a log trap. It was dark like this, she said, when they heard it—like a cougar screaming, had I ever heard that?—and they knew they'd caught it. They took the rifle and the kerosene lanterns and ran toward that awful sound, she said. And there it was, down in that pit.

What did they do then? I asked.

"Well, they killed it," she laughed. "It was a big one, too, a silvertip."

Then she told about how she and her sister Nettie had found the dead Indian. It was on the journey to Idaho, when they were sent out for wood to bring back to the wagons for the supper fire. She was eight, Nettie was ten. They knew he was dead, so they tried not to be afraid. They went closer. He was wearing beautiful buckskin clothes, she said. Decorated all over with beads. The moccasins were so pretty. Nettie was older, but she had been the one who reached out her hand. Then the bones rattled, and she dropped the moccasin and ran.

"We didn't tell until the next day," she said. "We thought we'd be in trouble. But Papa said if we'd told him he would have gone back and got us those moccasins. They had beads all over, even on the soles." She looked out her white lace curtains at the blackened street, and straightened the crocheted doilies on the arm of her chair. "You stay out of those woods," she told me. "You've got no business up on that hill."

The teachers smiled when they talked about the Nez Perce, who had helped Lewis and Clark build their canoes right here where our town is now. And we learned a new word: sesquicentennial. Katherine, who was not Nez Perce but Shoshone like the real Sacajawea, was beautiful in her beaded white buckskin dress. We knew how much it hurt to hold her arm up like that through the whole pageant, pointing the way. The rest of us girls sat at the back of the stage while the boys, one by one, walked into the West. Mike was a miner, Rick a farmer. Gary was a carpenter. We were squaws, the teachers told us. We weren't supposed to move.

It had taken Katherine's grandmother three years to make the dress. From the shadows at the back of the stage I watched as the family helped the old woman to her seat in the front row. The golden fringe of her many-colored shawl reached below her long dress, and another silk scarf covered her head. An older boy walked on each side of her as if she were made of snowflakes just before they touch each other.

Or like robin's eggshells, pieces of perfect blue I hung on the little pine trees by the gate, signals to something I felt in the air. They would be there for days, and then—I'd be listening to the mourning dove up on the hill, its question and its three-note answer, or watching the mullein rise along the road, and when I looked for them they would be gone.

The pageant happened after the winter of the pink snow. When we went out one morning the world was covered in pastel cotton candy. We ate some, but it tasted like the sky and wet jersey gloves, just like regular snow. "Snow ice cream!" said Jill. "We could have pink snow ice cream!" Our zippered boots tracked the magic snow onto the kitchen floor as we pushed through the door to ask Mom. Her hands were spreading a white circle of flour over the bread-board. We watched her face pale above our double handfuls of faintly pinkish snow. The snow, Mom told us, might be pink because of the atomic explosions. Maybe it was tiny pieces of Utah falling on us in Idaho, the dust of Utah's red rock. She made us take off our wet clothes and put our stockinged feet up on the open cookstove door while we drank our hot cocoa. "I guess I can't keep you inside all winter," she said when we begged to go back out. "But don't eat any more snow."

It was because of the war, she said. The pink snow.

One morning I found her at the kitchen table, her head laid on her arms, crying. Her back was shaking, vibrations that lifted my hand and made it shake too. "Mama?" The Korean War had ended, she said. No, we didn't have any uncles in this war. But other people did. She couldn't stop crying, even though the war was over.

7

Sometimes, down in the woods where the yellow pine trunks glowed red-orange in the afternoon hum of beetles, or lying on my back in the fern patch hideout and looking up through lace at a building thunderhead, I could almost hear the voices. I knew I was lucky to be here, closer to them than I would have been if we lived in a place of concrete sidewalks and wide, paved highways. When we learned in fourth grade Idaho History that our state's name came from the Ni Mii Pu words "Ee dah how! Behold, the sun comes rolling down the mountain!" I had closed my eyes and seen it: the sun lighting the tops of the pines a green we wouldn't see again all day, then the wave of color sliding down the ridge to find us as the shadows of the east field border-firs shrank back to their daylight size. I knew that we saw stars the way the Ni Mii Pu had seen them, in pure darkness, and we swallowed the same dusty huckleberries. The same chinook wind filled our mouths. I had seen the sunset filter through pine needles since I could remember. We had watched snow turn magic, crusting over until we could walk right over the top barbed wire, wearing nothing but Dad's wool socks over our shoes to keep us from slipping. Walking on diamonds.

But I wanted more. "To feel the earth as rough to all my length," like that poem by Robert Frost. To climb inside this place and hear its heartbeat against my own, to feel its breath coming into my own lungs, warm against my face, guiding my hands along the smoothing wood beneath my jackknife. I wanted to hear ninebark leaves and read the white buckberry's messages. I was still watching for them in the dark treeline at the edge of the east field. The Old Ones. Indians. What does it mean to be alive on this earth? I didn't think I could ever really know unless they spoke to me.

Meanwhile, the things I was learning in school spun like tops around me, careening suddenly across the surface of the home place and toppling crazily to one side. None of these lessons seemed to fit with the land I stepped down onto every afternoon when the school bus door opened—the sound of whitetail deer stamping their hooves or the smell of ferns and blackberries ripening by the gate. History had begun with Columbus—or for us, with Lewis and Clark. Indians had been Savages who attacked wagon trains with burning arrows, but were now a quiet embarrassment, people who wore the wrong clothes and had messy front yards. Like women—like what I would be, unless I could convince people I was almost a boy—they were never completely "grown up." They didn't realize that life is progress. The science book had plastic overlays of jet engines and hydroelectric turbines, each layer taking you deeper and deeper into what really mattered. My cousins from Washington taught us the song. "On up the river is Grand Coulee Dam / biggest thing made by the hand of a man / to run the great factories and water the land / roll on, Columbia, roll on!"

Dad talked about how beautiful this country used to be and how much it had changed, all the white pines gone now, he said. But the ads in the magazines thought it was good to cut the trees. Little seedlings grew right out of the stumps. One picture showed a black and white line of skunks, a mother and her kits, walking through a logged clearing. Looking for a home, the ad said. Just like people. And look: there is plenty of lumber here, enough for homes for everyone! None of the homes in the magazines looked like our family's, though. Ours was two rooms, just a little bigger than the old board shack, with a lean-to bedroom Dad had added on with more reject lumber from the planer mill where he worked at night. He called it a tarpaper shack, and even though he had built it for us with his new Skil saw, straightening the old nails from the Hills Brothers Coffee can and driving them in with only three blows of the hammer, I could tell he was ashamed of it. Having an outhouse was bad, too, and so was carrying water in buckets, though our well water tasted like spring air. I didn't know what we had done to be the wrong people. And I didn't understand why girls couldn't read *Boy's Life* and learn to tie knots and build canoes and make a model airplane that could really fly. There were so many questions we weren't even supposed to ask. What *was* Communism, and why was it red?

"Why aren't there any Negro people here?" I asked my mother, who had taught us that "niggertoes" and "olly olly ox in free ... (niggers up a tree!)" were words that meant something. Words we shouldn't say. But she didn't seem to know. People want their family and friends around them, she said. Of course, but they'd be here, wouldn't they?

9

"Next year you'll be taking PE," said one of my teachers. "How would you like to have to use the same towel a Negro had used?" It gave me the same feeling as the pictures of the stacked bodies I'd seen in one of the magazines, chests and legs so thin that I had mistaken bodies for fenceposts. I understood, then. This was an evil so big nobody could explain it, not even Mom.

The first time I saw a Black person I had stared from the window of the car where we sat waiting outside the medical clinic in Lewiston, fascinated by his hands—white on the inside!—but even more by his rumpled blue suit jacket. We didn't have TV yet, and except in the Dick and Jane readers, I had never seen a man wearing a suit jacket for everyday. In those pictures, the fathers who wore suits always had white cuffs emerging from the sleeves, and this man had only those magical hands, turning black and white as they moved. For one dizzying moment I thought maybe this mysterious evil was simply more fuss about people wearing the wrong clothes.

On this benchland above the Clearwater River in north-central Idaho where my grandfather had homesteaded—a latecomer, he had settled not on rich bottomland where he could earn a living but in these mountains taken from the Nez Perce Reservation after the Allotment Act—I would grow up off balance, moving in a kind of awkward dance through the sloping field of my questions. Long before I knew the word "politics" I was testing my schoolyard truths against my own first knowledge, looking across the pasture toward the log cabin and the place where the tepee had stood. I knew we were poor, though when we asked our mother about it she would explain that "poor" meant more than eating potato chips only on the Fourth of July and olives only on Thanksgiving, a lot more than wearing clothes handed down from our cousins and using the Christmas wrapping paper over and over. There were people, she said, who couldn't take their children to the doctor when they were sick, kids who didn't have winter coats or applesauce from the cellar for lunch. But why didn't everyone have a place to live, shelter against the wind, warm food, fire? How could such things be, when humans already knew how to survive, how to live well? It had happened—generations of ordinary people living ordinary lives with enough food and medicine for every child, and a

10

warm place to sleep—right here on the dirt where our potatoes grew. I ate a piece of it, something I couldn't quite name, every night at supper.

It has been more than fifty years since the log house burned and we were left standing in the center of the home place. My parents were shaken to the core, but they would work hard, like their parents before them, trying to make a good story. They wanted the same things everyone wants: to survive, to be loved, to find meaning in their lives. But there would be guns in our family's story, and quarrels over land and water that separated people who loved each other. There was isolation by class, by race, by gender. Sometimes by our own choices. And there were important pieces of the story—mental illness and suicide—that could not be spoken aloud. My grandparents' and parents' story has, of course, branched into my own, and mine has branched into my child's. Struggling to understand it, I realize that our family story is only a very small part of a much larger one. The American West, America itself, the colonizing of four continents. It's easy to get trapped in this bigger story where human bodies and the earth they stand on can become expendable resources, some parts to be grubbed out to make room for others.

My family would work from first light until after dark to keep the fences fixed, the wood split and carried and the lamps lit, the animals fed and milked, and the loose hay and garden produce put away for the long, deep snows. To make a home. When the pink snow fell around us, though, I sensed that the Cold War quarrels outside our house and the tensions inside it were like the ripples on the pond when I threw a pebble in—they were coming from the same center and growing bigger all the time. Near the end of his life my father grew bitter. "That place destroyed me," he said once. But our family shared joy on the home place too, and love; jokes and teasing and times when we just watched the moon together with no sound but the late summer crickets.

In my deep-sleep dreams, I am always on that land above the Clearwater. I would grow up to make mistakes of my own and feel the

11

pain of my own separations and losses, but I have always known that there is guidance in the land beneath my feet. It's stolen land. The hillside I was born into had been taken more recently than much of North America—only five decades before I was born—and the footprints of the people who had left that tepee ring were still visible. I knew from the beginning that stories stay in the earth. When you walk over them, their dust rises up as the bluebird lights the air above you.

Not long ago I was walking across the grass at the community college where I teach—in a town in Eastern Oregon just off the big river that carries the Clearwater to the Pacific—with one of my students, a young Indian woman. "Are you Indian?" Thea asked me suddenly. I don't look Indian. She may have meant: are you part Indian, even a small part? Were you raised in this way? Did you have a grandmother, an auntie, to teach you? Maybe it was something I had said in class, some angle of vision that felt familiar to her.

Or maybe she meant: why did you come here?

I opened my mouth to answer her, but I could not speak. How could I tell her? I wasn't there any longer, walking beside her. I was back on the home place looking up at the old yellow pine, a late-August sun setting through its needles, still rooted to the field, staring at something high in its branches. A swarm.

Dad had spoken to us for the first time in months. "Come with me." He had been angry all summer, a silent anger. It was the summer I was sixteen, the summer he had started drinking again. We followed his boots across the tilled earth, past the corn and through the potatoes, almost into the shadow of the pine. "They're swarming," he said. He shaded his eyes, looking up. "See them? About three feet from the top, on the south side." Yes, we told him, our voices a flood of relief. Yes, we see them. Then he left us in the field, and we heard the barbed wire squeak against the fence staple. We stood there, my younger brothers and me, children of this troubled father, staring into the light. The swarm was a golden halo above that echoing place in the earth, the place where I first understood that the earth was alive and that I was alive on the earth. Finally the light faded, suddenly gone behind the ridge, dropping the way it does in Idaho, leaving the pale orange sky, and I realized my brothers had gone back to the house. The bees were a cloudy silhouette now against the clumps of black pine needles, still keeping their queen warm at the center. In the morning, I knew, they would be gone. They were looking for a home.

# Land and the Language of Silence

🦋

My mother gave me the word that cracked the code: MILK. It was the first word on the Milk of Magnesia tin. "This is M," she said. "I. L. And K. Mmmm-illl-k."

And just like that, I was free.

My letters didn't sit as straight as my sister's on the thin blue line as we bent over this mystery, but each one made a sound. No more long lines of "e's" scrawled on the peeling gray wallpaper—this was really writing. COFFEE, Jill was copying from the red can. Oh. *Oh.* The world was full of words, waiting for me to find them. They perched in rows, like birds, whispering secrets.

I had found it. There was a way inside the stories I could feel moving all around me, breathing from the shadows at the edges of the pasture and sifting through the firs in the afternoon light. You could pull words right out of the air and lay them down on paper like footprints on snow. Then these footprints would lead—in a strange kind of magic I couldn't quite touch yet—to something that would connect the ragged edges, all those questions I didn't even know how to ask. Like Mama's darning needle connected the empty spaces in our socks.

"Circle the one that does not belong." My pencil drew sober gray balloons around the girl without a hair ribbon, the puppy with only one ear. *Why?* "That's how they do it in school," Jill said. We lay on our stomachs on the floor now, our heads almost touching. She was letting me in on the secrets of reading and writing, even though I was only four. But in the workbooks she brought home to share with me that winter, words were leading to mysteries of their own. By the time I had reached the long tables of first grade myself, I knew I was supposed to pretend that I didn't know "orange" or "airplane"—Mrs. Cole was cross if you could already hear the sounds of letters. Even in second grade, when it was okay to know how to read, Miss Simmons took the best book out of my hands and put it on her own desk. "You're not old enough for *Huckleberry Finn*," she said. "And it's giving you ideas."

So it was a forbidden power, like almost everything in the adult world. Maybe the best way to approach it was through a secret entrance. That summer, the last one before we would fall into the loops of cursive, my best friend Barbara and I were busy inventing codes of our own. You could write a message in milk and hold it over a flame, Barb said. (Jill and I tried this one together, our hearts pounding as the brown-streaked letters emerged above the stolen match.) Better yet, you could invent a Secret Code and keep the key hidden. I spent hours crouched in high, you-kids-stay-out-of-there places, like the loft of the freestanding building we called the cellar, its thick walls sweet with ancient insulating sawdust—I had to climb over the hot, tarpapered woodshed roof to get in—composing and decoding messages. In the slice of sun that came through the crack in the splintery door, I unfolded the paper that matched all twenty-six letters with the strange designs we had invented for each of them. I kept the coded key in an old Milk of Magnesia tin whose label softened against my jeans pocket and finally disappeared. Red-winged blackbirds called from the cattails in the draw, and log trucks downshifted to climb the grade into the afternoon as letters emerged from their hiding places and separated into words: "Dear 'Silver Starlight'." But the messages were a disappointment. "Come over tomorrow. OK?"

Could this be all? Wasn't there a code that could discover secrets worth knowing? I thought about that heart-shaped shadow Jill and I could just make out when we squinted through the thinning tan fabric on the back of Aunt Grace's old hand-cranked phonograph. We knew *he* must have put it in there, somehow—the boy Delbert who had loved the girl Grace even though they both knew his asthma would probably kill him. How did he ever get it inside this place with no entrance? Uncle Delbert had died when I was small, but it seemed if we could only reach that shadow we would finally know the answer to a real grown-up mystery: whatever it was they had known that had kept them laughing together. But when we finally pushed hard enough to rip the old fabric and reached through the torn place, all we pulled into the light was a small, empty candy-box lid, heavy with dust.

Violet-green swallows were circling outside, calling to each other. Beneath these deep shavings in the windowless cellar, whose thick

15

sawdust-filled walls kept the air cool even in summer, I know that my grandmother had once developed her first photographs with a red-muffled flashlight. I'd seen the pictures. They were curling and brown, but I could recognize the trees behind the barn and that boy in baggy knee pants who would grow up to be my father. How had she felt, I wondered, calling these shapes out of the darkness with only a dim light in her hand? But chemicals and flashlights couldn't explain my mother's eyes as she looked up from the venison steaks she was dipping in flour to check the color of afternoon light on the hillside pines and the line of western sky above them. Or the silence around my father's hands, one on each side of the green coffee cup; the sound of his chair pushing back from the table. The key, I was sure, was in the stories they started to tell but didn't really finish.

The Secret Code had worn to a soft-edged silence. I climbed down from the cellar loft and put the Milk of Magnesia tin back into the box that held my marbles and red flint and airplane cards. "Let's write stories to each other," Jill said. We had finished all our library books and the August afternoon would last forever. "The Mystery in the Old Barn," each of us wrote at the top of our pages, and our pencils whispered in the shadow of the fir tree.

"What are you doing?" my mother asked me that fall, when I came home from third-grade penmanship practice.

"I'm writing," I told her. My fingers wouldn't stop at the end of the blue-lined tablet. They kept tracing invisible letters in the air, reaching toward the words that hung, unspoken, all around us.

At the back of the bottom drawer where Mom kept her special things—I knew I shouldn't be looking there—I found a scrapbook. Mom had made scrapbooks for Jill and me, too: new-baby cards, locks of our first hair, tiny blue inked hand prints. This one was filled right up to the back cover with poems she had cut from magazines and pasted in. I pictured Mom in the little log cabin, a summer afternoon like this one, when she was "first married." Dust motes drifting in the air, her silver scissors curving around the borders of each poem. A secret scrapbook, just for herself.

"Silly," she called it now. She wasn't even upset with me. She set the sprinkling bottle on the table beside the basket of tightly rolled shirts and turned a few pages, her fingers still damp. I could tell she was reading. Smells mixed together in the kitchen, the sprinkled-clothes smell and the powdery smell; I'd found the scrapbook under her silky slip. "I was so young," she said. The poems were mostly about flower petals and drops of rain.

But there was another book of poems, too, part of a set of three books with cardboard bindings colored to look like old parchment. Classics Book Club, I read beneath their titles. There was no money for books in our house, but these three were like the "on approval" stamps I could order, bringing India and Egypt and Iceland into the fir-shaded dust of our own mailbox, right there with the smell of ferns and dog-fennel and the dry rustle of snake-grass, keeping the free samples as long as I sent back the "real" stamps. When I watched the way Mom's hands touched this book of poems, I knew she wouldn't call it "silly." *Palgrave's Golden Treasury.* At first I thought the title came from the shiny edges of the paper. Then I found it: "Oft have I traveled in the realms of gold ..." *Then felt I like some watcher of the skies / When a new planet swims into his ken.* I took a deep breath, as if I'd been under water a long time. It made me think of the way Mom had tilted back her head on that long ago night when she had first taken me outside to show me what lit the darkness above us.

Now her wrists were white with flour, her arms kneading, turning, kneading; pushing the rolling pin across the dough for pie crusts or biscuits or cinnamon rolls; or her hands glistened above the steam of the canner kettle or burned red against the laundry stick, forcing the scalding jeans and shirts and towels into the wringer; her hands folded around paring knives and diaper pins and onion skins and green beans and dishcloths and mop handles. Her hands could do anything. 17 Potatoes and refrigerator cookie dough sliced into perfect dominoes; peaches slipped their skins like moons. "It just takes practice," she told me.

One afternoon we found a package just the right size to fit in the mailbox, a square wrapped in brown paper and double-tied with white string. It was from Grammie. What did it mean? We stood there as the school bus rattled over the washboard place over by the rock crusher, and out of hearing. Jill pushed the string aside and touched the dark penciled address—"To BUD"—while Tom wobbled on his tiptoes, pulling her arm down so he could see too. I felt that hollow feeling, as if I'd missed the bus and it was coming dark, even though I was home, and all we had to do was walk down the hill, past the barn and the crabapple tree, and into the house. We set the package at Dad's end of the supper table and changed into chore clothes. He worked the day shift now, so he'd be home from the mill any minute.

When the taut string popped above his sharp blade and he folded the jackknife back into his palm, I saw that blade lifting a jagged splinter from my skin, and peeling an almost-ripe apple in straight green strips, stem end to blossom, instead of the curves and spirals of my mother's paring knife. I thought of the sharpened tips of the perfect double marshmallow sticks he held out to us. And I tasted metal, remembering the raw wood smell of a fresh-cut switch in his hand, after he'd closed the knife like he had just now. What did he hope would be in the box? He pushed back the brown paper and opened the box to a white surprise—rows of our grandmother's sugar cookies. They were his favorites: she always used real sour cream, and the cookies were extra thick. They always felt like feather pillows and clouds inside my mouth; they could make me forget all about chocolate.

But they weren't as thick as the sounds coming from his throat, his words ripping, burning their way out into the air; or as thick as his fingers jerking knots into the broken string, pulling it into a tight stranglehold around the box. With a blunt pencil stub, he wrote in black letters—so much like hers—PACKAGE REFUSED.

Then we watched him carry the box back up the long driveway, his boots not slowing even where the hill steepened.

The quarrel was about the ranch we were living on. We had moved back onto the place when I was six months old, after Dad's parents had moved to town and his father had been partially paralyzed by a stroke. Mom told us that she and Dad had wanted to buy land of their own, but my grandparents needed them here to keep up the home place—and besides, my grandfather had told them, "You don't want to end up on some little scrub piece of hillside." So when Dad came home from his job at the mill he still had another job to do: plowing and fertilizing and seeding the alfalfa fields, putting in the garden, stringing barbed wire and pounding fence posts, feeding and milking and shoveling snow from the roofs of the outbuildings, cutting and raking and shocking and hauling in the hay, and tossing it, heavy forkfuls, down the square opening from the dark loft into the winter lantern light and the circle of thick-furred barn cats around the battered dish, waiting for the froth-warm milk. The place would be his some day, his parents had promised, if he'd just live there and take care of it for them. And meanwhile, though there was still no money to be made from this kind of subsistence ranching—and he would be paying those steady bills, too, for feed and fertilizer and broken machinery—the homestead would feed his children as it had theirs. Land prices were still low, and Dad and Mom had wanted to buy the ranch, but no, no need for that. "Just treat it as if it's yours," Dad's father had said. But now—I was ten, we'd been here all this time—his father was gone. Almost immediately a neighbor asked Grammie if she would sell the place. Had that put the idea in her head, or had she been thinking of this before? Its value had tripled. She offered the ranch to Dad's younger brother, our Uncle Joe who lived in California. When he said no, she put the place up for sale.

Was she worried about money now that our grandfather was gone? As far as I knew, she had the same veteran's pension she'd always had, and some income from his family's Washington wheat crop—that other long-standing family conflict over land resolved at last—and if she needed anything, Dad would know. He had been the son who stayed close to help his parents, all those Sunday visits ... Maybe it wasn't fair, just one son getting the ranch? But his brother's and sisters' inheritances from the wheat ranch and the sale of her house would be about the same value. And they wanted Dad to have it. I'd heard all this hashed over at great length by now. So I knew what was really

19

killing my father. Dad thought she meant that there was no place in her world for him—this first son who, no matter what he did, just wasn't the child she had wanted.

I wondered what he thought she meant by sending the cookies.

Gravel spilled out from the edges of his stride as he came back down the driveway, looking across the field where he'd grown up following the team around the stumps of the huge yellow pines. When his head turned back toward the house I stepped quickly away from the window. Can mothers really stop loving their children? By the time he reached the porch my arms were heaped with stovewood, and the box was half full.

Lunch box messages were a language any kid could read. Maybe he was just too tired to notice that Mom kept filling his lunch box with the ginger creams he loved so much—she made a few gingerbread men for my younger brothers, but cut most of the dough into the round shapes that would fit beside his sandwiches. Remember, I told myself, he's been lifting lumber at the planer mill all day. But I knew it was more than that. He didn't come in from chores and kiss Mom on the back of the neck any more. Sometimes after he had unlaced his boots and turned toward the supper table, he didn't raise his eyes above his plate, except to look down the table to ask for more bread. On those nights I thought the five of us, five children circling his table— the little boys squeezed together on the bench in the back—must be heavy, a weight pushing on the back of his neck. When I stood beside the chopping block waiting for his axe to fall into the seam that would split the wood blocks into chunks, I watched his face, the places he held so still at other times. And I followed him to the barn, helping him spread load after load of manure over the east field and the garden. He buried the strawberries under shovelfuls of it, working at a pace that made my back and arms burn trying to keep up. We were buying the ranch. He had surprised his mother by walking into the real estate office with the thousand-dollar down payment in his hand. It was money saved, of course, at a terrible cost. "We'll just move away," Mom had urged him. "We'll find another place to live." But he wouldn't.

20

And how could he? How could any of us live without the smell of this air? Would the sun roll down the mountain and warm our faces anywhere else? How could we sleep without the river-sound of wind swaying those big yellow pines up on the hill? Yet making the payments to his mother was twisting him like the dishtowels Mom wrung dry, as our poverty bit deeper. He was our father, the man who worked so hard and stood between us and danger, but he was someone else too. Who was this man who had beaten Tom so savagely that afternoon when he walked down the street from his first-grade classroom after school to Grammie's house and didn't make it back in time to catch the bus? Stay away from her, Dad had told us. And from our favorite aunt, my mother's best friend since high school—and the cousins who felt more like sisters, the ones in all the pictures of us kids lined up on Grammie's porch steps squinting at the camera, the ones whose look-alike dresses Jill and I had been inheriting all our lives. What could she have done, Aunt Edie? Maybe she hadn't tried hard enough to argue Grammie out of her new idea, as the other aunts and Uncle Joe had; or maybe she had said something like, "Remember, Bud, she's still upset about losing Dad. Be gentle with her, come talk to her." We didn't know. And we didn't dare ask. When Mom had tried to argue he had flailed like a drowning person losing his hold on the last floating piece of wreckage. We were afraid of this new father, and we were even more afraid of watching him disappear under this whitewater. So there would be no more family picnics under the fir tree. Soon he stopped speaking to our neighbors—the people who had always called on him to fix the party telephone line when it sagged and broke under the weight of wet snow—or even raising his two-finger salute from the steering wheel. People in cars we didn't know slowed down when they drove by our place as if they were trying to find us, see anything they could still recognize.

Section 27, Township 37, Range 3 east. The small yellow plate is still nailed to a tree at the corner of the east field, telling its story in numbers and straight lines scribed into metal. What would our lives have been like, I wonder, if our family had shared the Nez Perce's stunned despair at the idea of dividing trees and rocks and rivers and even the June perfume of syringa into these imaginary squares? "You

21

are trifling with the laws of the earth," their spokesman Toohoolhoolzote had told General Howard when he ordered the Wallowa Valley band to the reservation at Lapwai. "The earth is part of my body ... What person pretends to divide the land, and put me on it?" But Howard had him thrown in the brig, and a decade later Senator Dawes would argue that partitioning the earth into small parcels, one for each man, was just what the Nez Perce and other Indian people needed. The problem with Indian cultures, Dawes said, was simple: "There is no selfishness, which is at the bottom of civilization." The Allotment Act and private ownership of land, he said, would change all that.

The strawberries burned under all that manure. That summer the alfalfa came up green, though, and Dad traded shifts with another man at the mill so he could hay all day and load boxcars at night. His neck blazed from red to bronze, darker and darker. And then his hair— the hair that made people ask if he were Indian—fell out, in dollar-sized patches. He felt it first. We had just come in to wash up for lunch. *No.* But he could see it, in the little round shaving mirror that hung on the wall beside the kitchen sink. "Look at me!" he said, his voice like rock salt. We watched as his hair dropped in handfuls and then grew back in rough patches of white and dull black, like a scrub pinto pony. He sat at the end of the kitchen table late into the night, cradling his coffee. We were careful not to make sudden noises or laugh out loud.

When I started seventh grade I played the cornet. Here was a whole new language. I practiced in the little fruit-cellar that Dad had built inside one corner of the sawdust-walled cellar. Music had a smell: valve oil and dirt-cellar squash. Potatoes. On the shelves the jars of corn and beans and peaches promised good things, a rainbow of colors. Night after night I practiced my solo—"Can't Help Lovin' That Man of Mine"—until my fingers were too cold to warm against the hanging light bulb. "Fish gotta swim, and birds gotta fly, I've gotta love that man 'til I die ..."

"No, no," said my band teacher, hitting his baton on the music stand as I lowered my horn. "You have to *feel* it."

One day when I set my stack of books on the kitchen table and let myself sink into the smell of the supper kitchen and Mom's voice, lifting the load of junior high for a few minutes before chores, she handed me a poem. "Mom, make lots of ginger men!" the small boy in the poem said, leaning over the cutting board, his brown eyes begging. Words danced across the page in delicate lines. Bluebirds and the shape of the skyline, small boys in red winter coats and white flour and the squeak of the kitchen floor. I looked up. She was looking out the window, toward the mailbox.

At the bottom of the page, the editors of the *Ladies Home Journal* had written, "We would like to publish your poem, but we need your permission to print your name." *Anonymous*, Mom had written beneath the poem.

"Are you going to do it?"

"No," she said. "I was hoping they'd print it without a name."

After three years of living in the almost the same kind of poverty we heard about in Mom's stories of the Great Depression, a letter had arrived from Grammie's lawyer: she had decided to deed the place to my father after all. He would henceforth have no further claim on her estate, the letter said. He had stared at the paper, put it down, and walked outside. Everything had changed, and yet nothing would change; we were still trapped inside my father's silence. I wasn't sure why, but I knew that Dad and his mother would never sit down and talk to each other, or listen. Or cry. It had been our family's land for three generations now, but we didn't know how to connect rocks and sky and children, roots and honey and the hunter who walks across the night sky. We didn't know the language.

Once I heard a young Indian man describe how he had deliberately refused to learn to read and had quit school as soon as he could. He had a world—worlds—to learn, and he resented the time locked inside the flattened walls of classrooms. But more importantly, he said, he feared the step back from fire and snow and the powdery language of moles, that distance between printed word and event. He didn't want to become like us. The People of the Book.

I knew what he meant, or thought I did. But even as I listened, my fingers moved in the air, still reaching. In my first winter at the University of Idaho I spent hours wandering the stacks in the library, letting my hand trace the spines of all those books, pulling them open, just touching their pages. Some had titles so dim I couldn't read them in the shadowy light. It hadn't been easy, getting to college. But it was inevitable. I could no more have made the choice that Indian man had made than a seed could have refused to sprout toward the sun.

I had the first year paid for. I'd sold the Hereford cows and their calves, the ones I'd bought with my 4-H steer money for this purpose. And I had the one small scholarship available in our high school, two hundred fifty dollars from Potlatch Forests, the very people who had kept my father laid off at the mill most of the winter. How I would pay for the next year I didn't know. But I could not have *not* gone, any more than I could have quit breathing. For years I'd been sneaking away from study halls and class projects to climb the stepladder in the high school storage room, perching up there in the dust to read the old literature books. At college a person could read all of them—and find the designs, that invisible spider webbing that held the stories together. Mothers and sons and fathers and daughters, sunrise and crescent moon, rain rising to flood for all those years, the western wind, that pulse of human terror and joy. There would be people at the university who knew these secrets.

That fall my English professor had held my first paper above the desk between us and asked me, "Who is it at home who's been to college? Someone at your house loves words. Who sent you on this journey?"

I shook my head: no, no one's been to college. He waited. "My mother," I told him. "And her mother, too, I think. But I'm the one who got to come."

Then on November 22 President Kennedy was shot. I couldn't join the others circled around the dorm's TV; all the words I heard there seemed wrong. I'd been learning about tragedy, but we had no Sophocles to shape this story. I sat with my back against a white birch in the arboretum, holding my books. On November 23 my mother's letter arrived: "By the time you read this I will be coming out of surgery. If it's cancer, he'll remove the breast. Radical mastectomy, they call it."

24

Everyone was saying they'd close school early and send us home for Thanksgiving. But words had already begun to fail us. How many days did it take for John Kennedy's body to disappear into the earth? Finally it was over. I caught a ride home with a friend who had a car, and it seemed like someone else's voice that I heard asking her to let me off at the hospital. Even in the silence that replaced the happy voices of students going home for Thanksgiving, I couldn't tell her why. I could not speak.

The little verse my mother mailed me in the fall of my sophomore year she had clipped from *The Farm Journal.* "Poems by farm wives." It wasn't one of Mom's—it had been written by some kindred-spirit sister—but I knew exactly what my mother was telling me.

### The Happy Mood

*It's lovely, and it's mine*
*and I shall not expose it*
*to the wind, the weather*
*or the world's comments.*
*In a green-edged corner*
*of my heart, I'll enclose it*
*with mist and moonbeams—*

*and it needn't make sense.*

I taped it to my dorm room door, beside the small picture of the single clover she had clipped to accompany the poem. If the cancer didn't recur immediately, the doctor had told her after she had finished the radiation treatments, she could expect to live five more years. When she had opened her eyes that November day a year before to a maze of tubes draining an empty hole in her chest, she had talked to my father for a long time. "It was the anesthetic," she told me later. "The things I said!"

25

What? What words had swirled in that closed hospital room? Something about the boys, she remembered—how they were too little to lose a mother. "You have to be *good* to them," she told him.

"Do you think she will live?" I had asked my father. The sound of my words surprised me. We sat on each end of the truck's bench seat, holding up her absence. His hands were white on the steering wheel, and the rusted ferns leaned toward us from the road bank. We were almost home.

"I have to believe she will," he said. He didn't look at me. "I have to believe that."

His words spread around me like water.

The pectoral muscle on her right side was gone—radical, at the root— but after a year she began making bread again, needing the rhythm of that heartbeat, knead, turn, knead, as much as she needed to regain the use of her right arm. The second poem she showed me was about the strength of this mystery, the secret kinship of women at the heart of the grain.

I looked at the words, her delicate l's and t's rising from the ends of the lines like feathered tips of wings. For some reason I thought of the radio Dad had brought home on that long-ago Valentine's Day, the magical hot-tube smell when I leaned close to the speaker, and the sound of Mom's voice as she dusted the breadboard with flour, singing along with the radio in the kitchen. "It's beautiful," I said.

It took a long time. But she recovered, and I was nearly through the university when her letters began to tell me a new story. Grammie had fallen through her cellar trapdoor and all of her children had been summoned to the hospital. And my father had gone. But nothing was broken after all, the doctor told them when they gathered at her bedside. She would live. Until now, the two youngest boys in our family hadn't known they had a grandmother, and Grammie had never seen my ten-year-old brother. *I take my lunch to her house, and we eat our sandwiches together at her big table*, Mom's letter said. Mom had been bitter too, of course, but she had long since learned the cost of hatred. Now she was prying apart the crack in the sealed wall we had been living behind for so long. And typing up the family stories Grammie was telling her—about walking beside the wagon all the way to Idaho, about the tent they lived in that first winter, about the summer she and her sister Nettie and the four other children from the tent families had gathered at the Schoolhouse Springs, learning to read and write.

26

Finally, just before Christmas, Mom sent a photo. There was Dad, sitting beside her at the end of the familiar maroon couch in Grammie's living room, his right arm stiff on the white doily. I held the picture for a long time. Mom was sitting very close to Dad. She was looking at him, her smile white in the glare of the flash, and her hand was resting on his knee. She was trying to rewrite this story, I knew. Give him back his mother, the small, dark woman behind the lens. Dad stared hard at something just to the left of the camera. Fudge and divinity and plates of my grandmother's Christmas cookies filled the coffee table in front of them, but my father's hands were empty.

When my father died, just before sunrise on a clear July morning in 1988, my parents had been married for fifty-one years. Mom had already outlived her own medical prediction by two decades, and she had spent the last five of those years nursing my father through the long agony of emphysema. What language was he speaking, that last morning of his life? After all those years together, what would he give my mother to hold on to? He lay on his back in the little bed, facing the window and the top of the ridge where in a few minutes—just after he was gone—the pines would catch the first touch of sun. "Don't get between me and the light!" he told her. And then, less sharply: "Go back to bed. Try to get some rest."

One of Mom's poems hangs on the wall in her kitchen, next to the window where she looks out to check on the mountain, the deer and goldfinches and flickers, and the fog above the river. Dad, I know, never saw it—or knew that she wrote poems at all.

It's a warm August morning, and throaty calls of ravens float through the screen door from the timbered hill above us. I'm watching the sun climb the bookcase, coloring the old paperbacks I mailed home one by one from college; and the larger books, direct from the library's New Books shelf, their plastic covers reflecting the light. Jill is the town librarian. Although the language of law had been her first choice, it was disappointing. It couldn't return the eleven-year-old daughter, adopted out to whites at birth, to the White Mountain Apache mother who sat in her Legal Aid office month after month. In the end, she would come back to the home place and these first stories.

27

Mom and I have been talking about regrets.

"The poetry was something I kept just for me," she says now. *I shall not expose it to the wind, the weather, and the world's comments.* I lift the cup my mother has poured me and breathe in the spice of this morning's tea. I think of that other summer morning, when I had just come home with a summa cum laude degree in English and a teaching contract for September, my woodbox filled with letters—all A's. It seems so simple now: I could do it this time. I'd be sitting next to him in the old kitchen, both of us cradling coffee cups now, and when he said, "You should have majored in math—then you could have gotten a *good* job, working for Boeing," I'd just lean over and kiss him on the forehead—did I ever kiss my father?—and say, "I love you, Dad, and I'll never stop loving you." It would be that easy.

But it hadn't been that easy then. What angry words had sputtered out of my mouth? *Math? Boeing? Jesus, Dad!* All I can really remember is his face, that look of stunned bewilderment. What had he said?

Mom is looking at me. "There are things I would do differently," she says. Her fingers touch the glass of milk, tracking a light line down the side. She's so small now. Milk, she says, is sometimes the only thing that still tastes good. "I didn't always try to break through."

I take her hand. These slender fingers that had curved around my own hand to guide the pencil, those small letters dipping between capitals and dancing in careful steps along the line. I wonder if she knows how hard I tried to make my letters just like hers, or how my hand is still trying to shape the vessel that will hold the words, the right words, the way the hand cups around the face of someone you love, the way I used to reach for my son's cheek at the dinner table when he was seven and eight, behind him that collage of photos on the wall (holding the dripping frog, running with the puppy, gazing into the trees), none of them quite catching his magic, my hand too not quite able to touch what I see in his cheek, just there under the temple ... In any of our languages, the mysteries slip through our cupped hands like water. Does she know how grateful I am for her brimming dipper of words? I lie beside her, on the nights when I visit— after we have talked far into the darkness—and listen to the sounds she speaks even in her sleep.

28

# Looking for Home

When an Indian man or woman stands up to speak at a public event in our community, what we hear first is an explanation of who is speaking. These are my parents, these people were my grandparents; this is where they were born, and they lived on this creek or river; I am of the Walla Walla and Cayuse people, or Nez Perce, Ni Mii Pu. This is my Indian name.

It must have been a kind of yearning for some part of what these speakers take for granted that I was searching for in those silent months after my extended family split apart the summer I was ten. Who were my people? What had led us to this place and then torn us all apart? I lay on my back in the pasture behind the house, hidden in a nest I'd made in the dense stems of narcissus that had come up there. Clouds blew overhead so fast it made me dizzy, and the smell of the flowers was like a food I could almost swallow. Their red and yellow cores were so small and bold in the center of that whiteness. All that had survived the fire when the log house burned were my grandmother's old flower beds, these bulbs buried deep in the February earth. By now the narcissus had spread to a big circle and grown high enough to shelter me from the house. I had picked up a triangular shard of broken cup or bowl with just enough of its faded colors left to make me wonder about the design. When Mom called for supper, I didn't move. I would just stay here in Grammie's old flowers, I thought, even though since we didn't go to visit her any more I probably shouldn't be here enjoying her flowers either. Or maybe that was silly. I was sure of only one thing: the quarrel that had made my family so unhappy was about who belonged here. I wanted to lie in my circle of spring until I felt the earth around me like my mother's arms. "Supper's ready!" Mom called again.

Years later, I am still looking for that feeling. Can I say my own name aloud and feel the earth beneath it? What got me up and out of my green shelter when I was a kid was knowing that it might be one of

29

those rare nights when my parents would stay at the table talking after supper was over, Dad's Lucky Strike smoke drifting over our plates, and I would hear stories, small pieces of the lives that had come before us.

The patterns were never clear to me. So many corners were broken off in the telling. But they had all been looking for a home, I could tell that much. Some of them had come to Idaho by wagon train, some by train, some bumping along in borrowed open cars with no coats, limping from blowout to blowout like the Joad family, piling out to trudge up the hills beside the car, pushing on the really steep grades. Some of them had walked away from the places of their birth as cleanly as if all the houses had burned behind them, leaving only the faint odor of ashes for us to sift for shards. And did they know what they were looking for, I wondered? How to recognize its shape? Some of them, like my mother's paternal grandparents, just kept moving. "Oh, he was just fiddle-footed," Mom tells me when I ask why a cabinetmaker had never settled into a fold of land where the grain of the wood spoke to his hands. Some of them came looking for gold ("I don't know why they believed Uncle Will; he was always a terrible liar ..."). Some of them came to claim the rights of kinship with others who had come before them; some, like my grandmother Emily, had come because there was nowhere else to go when she discovered that she didn't belong where she was. Would her real mother claim her, when she found her at last? It must have been a long journey.

Sometimes, after they got here, they moved away and then came back again. From the stories told at the supper table I learned that both of my parents had left the Clearwater River as small children but had circled back to grow up here after all. Their families had returned exhausted, in grief and pain and even deeper poverty, but the land had gathered them in like any mother whose children have strayed.

30

What all the journeys had in common was that mixture of desperation and hope. They may have also shared the spark so common to immigrants, the one we don't glamorize in our history lessons. Greed. But their main goal, at least the one I could hear most clearly in the dim-whispered stories, was sheer survival.

Maybe that's why I made a story to cover the bad taste that had filled my mouth when my mother told me about the Allotment Act. We had this land because the Nez Perce had lost part of their reservation, she said. But we were different, I told myself. We weren't like the soldiers who had killed little Indian kids with their bayonets and given the old men blankets loaded with smallpox. We weren't even like the town kids with their stitched-down pleated skirts and matching sweater sets. They're the ones who took the land away, I thought—and they only let the poor people, the latecomers, settle on the leftover pieces of it: the steep, rocky places that would keep them poor. We were more like Indians. Our ancestors had been poor people too, refugees. Our name was Lynch, an Irish name. My great-grandfather Gus had left Ireland after that land had failed to feed its own people—when the people who came to rule the land decided its native people were "vermin," a "lower race" clinging to ancient superstitions. Two million people starved, their bellies swollen and their mouths green from trying to eat grass, while the gifts of their country's soil were shipped to others. "Nits make lice." When the children of Ireland died, didn't the owners of the land there say the same thing Colonel Chivington had said after killing Cheyenne children at Sand Creek, or what the mob of eight hundred men in Jacksonville, Oregon, said when they hanged a seven-year-old Modoc boy? I could read about it in the schoolbooks. "A Modest Proposal." It was supposed to shock us. "If they're so hungry, let them eat their own children." And Mom's family, too—refugees from the highlands of Scotland, from Wales, escaping oppression and the revenuers, pushing the still that had kept bread in the children's mouths over the cliff just in time ... Even my grandparents, one on each side, had been orphaned, abandoned.

But the truth turned out to be more complicated. When my mother  31
began researching her family's history long after I was grown, a photograph arrived in the mail of an apparently Indian man holding his small son—an older brother of the one who would grow up to be so "fiddle-footed"—on his lap. The family knew the man's name and birthplace (Surrey County, North Carolina; 1828), but nothing except the face in the photograph suggested that he was Indian. This man

was the first of our family to come west, in a wagon train to California in 1848. But he had turned north, going all the way to Oregon's Willamette Valley, where he stopped at the foot of the Cascades near what would become the town of Sweet Home. Then he went out to gather wood for the long dark rains ahead and was mauled by a bear. It took him three weeks to die.

Someone had traced the family of his widow, the mother of two small boys now, back to a man "of strong Puritanical leanings, like his brother the regicide," who had come to America in 1643. "Scarce had he set up his rooftree in the wilderness when hardships and exposure struck him down," read the photocopied pages. This man's son Henry had grown up to die in the spring of 1676, when "the Indians, led by King Phillip of Mount Hope, Rhode Island, made a general war on the white settlements."

By then I was old enough to understand that no one is innocent. Those presences I had first sensed as a small child—glimpses of a land alive with spirit—were not something I had earned by being different from other white "settlers" on Indian land. And really, I had known it even then. They were a gift, like grace.

Most of the journeys to Idaho had been fairly recent. Dad's parents had both come as children. Grammie Alice's covered wagon train in 1897—five or six Missouri sharecropping families looking for a better life—must have been one of the last caravans. Her parents, Sarah and Milton, were forty-six and forty-seven; their oldest daughters were already young widows with children, and their youngest child was five. Alice was seven the year they started. Where the roads were washed out, she said, they traveled on the railroad tracks, with someone stationed ahead and behind them to flag the trains, which would stop and give them time to get off the ties. No one rode in the wagon on those days, she laughed. Besides, she told me when I was a child, she wanted to be able to say she had walked all the way. Or am I just imagining this memory, those small legs? They stopped each weekend so the men could trade work for horse feed with farmers along the way, and her mother would do the washing. By fall they had made it to Sturgis, South Dakota. Today my cousin rolls into Sturgis on her Harley for the annual August party, but in 1897 our grandmother and her family were wintering in a farmer's sod house where they burned buffalo chips against the deep cold; they found his barn to help with morning chores by following a rope through the blizzards.

Alice's mother and father had yearned for a home so deeply that they climbed into the wagon behind Prince and Dick not once but twice to leave behind their past and their future too, some of their own children and grandchildren. Minnie and her three children were still back in Missouri, now Jennie and her baby would stay here in Sturgis; Jennie had married the farmer's son. Alice remembered her mother's light bread, set to rise in the Dutch oven as they traveled and baked to a lovely brown in the bed of coals each night, and the gatherings around the campfire to sing "the good old Methodist songs." Her little brother Allen was still worried about his hat, lost when they were crossing the river at Chicago, the Windy City. She told us about dropping the dead Indian man's moccasin when the bones inside it rattled, but there were other stories too, less haunting. The chocolate coffee the two bachelors gave her after supper, along with rolls of fine baby ribbon she and her sister saved for their dolls, using the raveling for thread. (Why did the two bachelors have baby ribbon, I wondered?) By fall they had made it to the Palouse country of eastern Washington and north-central Idaho. While the men worked the wheat harvest, Sarah and her daughters collected food. Farmers gave them hundred-pound sacks of prunes and apples; there were green beans and even pumpkins hanging on strings to dry.

Not until the fall of 1899 would they arrive in Orofino, the city of gold. Despite Uncle Will's big promises, there are no stories of trying to mine. Idaho's gold rush, which had lasted only long enough to dispossess the Nez Perce, was long over. They lived through the winter in a tent house along the Clearwater—there were several tent houses there, my grandmother said—and again she briefly got to go to school, as she had on the Palouse. That spring they filed their homestead claim for 160 acres above Whiskey Creek, on the benchland just below the one her future husband would homestead and where I would grow up. And then they set about changing the land.

33

It was still going on when I was a small child. Dad was dynamiting the last of the stumps. Once we heard an explosion so big and a silence so loud that my mother gathered Jill and me in her arms to hurry across the pasture and through the draw, panting up over the rise of the east field where we found him coming to meet us. His face was streaked with dirt and laughter, hers with tears.

They had been huge, these old-growth yellow pines. Her family had worked from dawn until ten or eleven at night, my grandmother told us. Falling, stacking and, because there were no mills yet to sell them to, burning the trees in huge piles. They grubbed the serviceberry brush too, pronouncing it "sarvis" as we still do today, piling it on the flames. It's the only time in her story that Alice spoke of hardship. They were living in the tent house at first, then a small frame house just big enough for two beds and a stove, a table and chairs. Sarah would set her bread to rise and leave her stew bubbling on the stove; when they would come in for dinner, Indians would be there, waiting quietly to share this meal. Alice's mother fried the bread the way Mom did on days when we worked outside, that golden crust and soft warm center. Maybe the Nez Perce men sat on the edges of the beds, if there wasn't room for everyone at the table. "Mother would give them whatever she had and they would leave," Grammie told us. "They weren't hostile. They never hurt us. But us kids were always scared to death of them."

I tried to picture it—the stacks of orange-barked logs, the heaving horses, and sweat-stained shirts. Sarah's face, lined with exhaustion. The roar of flames. What did those Nez Perce men think as they waited, watching?

"It was a regular wilderness," Grammie said. "There were rattlesnakes—big ones, five or six feet long. We had to kill them with the hoe."

34

Already they knew this wasn't farmland, though they would "stump ranch," plowing the clay soil around the stumps for two generations to grow hay for the team and a milk cow, building up a few steers for meat if things went well. Growing a garden. They knew the men would have to continue to leave home to work in the Palouse harvests or make cordwood to trade down in the town for calico and flour and shoes. Later, Alice's husband Charlie, and his boys—my dad and Uncle Joe—would work in the woods. As a young man, my dad would hike out of the logging camps every Saturday night and back in on Sunday with groceries for the week, but when his own father began working in the woods there were only two days off, at Christmas. That first year on the Idaho homestead Alice and her brothers and sister had to gather dry ferns and add a little grain to keep the horses, Prince and Dick, alive.

In the spring the younger children, Alice and Nettie and their brother Allen, went to school for three months in a neighbor's house and then the men built a log school on the half bench above them at Schoolhouse Springs. Fourteen-year-old girls taught the younger children. But with winter snows four or five feet deep the school terms were short. They all traveled for miles—clear over to Harmony Heights—for picnics, dancing on the puncheon floor of somebody's house until daybreak, everyone tired and happy in the wagon coming home. And Alice walked with Allen to the neighbors, selling needles to earn a watch she would keep pinned to her dress, a watch as big as a man's. They timed their visits so they arrived at the bachelor John Wells' house just in time for his sourdough biscuits.

Two years after they had claimed their homestead, Milton, who was fifty-two by this time, and his boys hewed logs for a house, and the neighbors came for a house raising. In all the pictures of my grandmother's family, this house is not just background. It is holding them up. "People were still living in that house in 1965," Alice liked to say. The house wasn't visible from the road, but I could see Milton and Sarah's headstones in the cemetery at the top of the Weseman grade every night from the school bus window. Pearl Weseman was the first neighbor girl to teach school. Then the bus angled up the ridge and turned back onto the shelf of hillside still called Wells Bench.   35

When Alice was thirteen, she rode the merry-go-round at the Fourth of July picnic for hours with Lawrence Mulvaney. They had been neighbors in Missouri and come out on the wagon train together. The summer she was sixteen, though, she was with another handsome young man at the dance, and when they married a few months later Lawrence Mulvaney left home and his family didn't hear from him for years.

Charlie Lynch. In the picture taken at the dance, all the girls wear white summer dresses, and Charlie is a man in love. "They were still lovers when I met them," my mother tells me. "After your Uncle Joe left home, Charlie would dry dishes for her after supper, and once I said, 'You two are on a second honeymoon,' and they both laughed."

By the time I knew him he had been partially paralyzed by a stroke and was a mostly silent man sitting all day in his chair. His dark bedroom smelled like sickness. Sometimes he went away to the Veterans' Hospital and Grammie cried. Once after I had stayed overnight, sleeping in Grammie's bed (in one of her slips; "don't slip in your sleep"), she handed him a plate of fried eggs and little orange slices and said, "I just hope you die first." She was having a fight, a yelling argument, but my grandfather hadn't spoken. He looked down at his eggs. I couldn't eat any breakfast.

This picture of my grandparents—the bent, silent man, the dark and bitter little woman wearing lace-up heeled shoes—is all I have, but of course it was not all there was.

When Charlie was two, his mother died in childbirth. She was twenty-six. I grew up holding her in my mind, our lost woman. Beautiful Belle Laird. Gus Lynch left his young sons with her parents in Michigan and came west to Washington, an Irish muleskinner running a freight line. When he had married again and settled down to farm in the Kittitas country, Charlie and his older brother Mace would join him. The first ten years of Charlie's life were the good ones, his grandfather Jonas a kind man. After that, things were hard. The story was sketchy. Troubles with the stepmother, leaving home at twelve to work for his keep. His first job was thinning carrots for the neighbors. Kneeling in our own garden when I was twelve, the needle shapes of carrots withering beside me in the sunlight, I tried to imagine being on my own.

At seventeen he went to the Philippines in the Spanish-American War. He wasn't in any battles, Dad told us. But Dad kept a billy club in his dresser drawer, a trophy from a barracks fight with Filipinos. It was stained with blood that had blackened with age. "He took this away from a nigger policeman," Dad said.

The billy club was smooth against my hand in the quiet summer afternoon when, alone in the house, I slid Dad's dresser drawer open and lifted it out. It was heavy. My mother hated it, and she hated the way Dad told the story. I wondered if she thought about it being so close to her head when she was trying to sleep.

Years later, I would read about the war in the Philippines, which lasted three years. The U.S. sent seventy thousand troops and the heavy casualties among them did not even begin to compare with the suffering among the Filipino people. One senator put it this way: "It has been charged that our conduct of the war has been cruel. Senators, it has been the reverse ... Senators must remember that we are not dealing with Americans or Europeans. We are dealing with Orientals." Another volunteer from Washington wrote, "Our fighting blood was up, and we all wanted to kill 'niggers.' ... this shooting human beings beats rabbit hunting all to pieces."

I slid the billy club back under the red bandanas. But my hand still remembered its shape. Nobody had said whose blood it was, I told myself. Maybe the policeman had hit someone and Charlie just took it away. Maybe it wasn't the policeman's blood. Why was this the only story passed down from those browning pictures that hung on the dark walls of my grandfather's bedroom, long lines of men standing perfectly still?

Charlie's half brother and sister would get to go to college, but when he returned from the Philippines he went to work in the wheat harvest, and that's where he met Alice's older brother. They joked about marrying each other's sisters, but when he followed his friend to Idaho and found Alice, it was for real. He staked a homestead claim on the bench of former Nez Perce land above Alice's family where he liked the lay of the land.

By the time my father was born there were three older sisters, and in the pictures the fields are full of stumps. Charlie had built a log house and an open-front log garage and what we would call "the old log chicken house." But the stories that follow Charlie, who spent so many days in the woods on one end of a crosscut saw, are not about log burnings but about trees—the corner woods, the barnyard firs, and the rim of ponderosa and fir that circled the east field. "The Old

37

Man wouldn't let anybody cut these," Dad said. "They were real special to him." When I was ten and had to have a tooth pulled, I stood under the barnyard firs and listened for my grandfather's courage. He had had all his teeth pulled with no anesthetic, Dad told us. I touched the rough bark, pressing my hand into its creases.

My father was six when his family left the home place. For two years they lived on Gus Lynch's farm in the Kittitas country of eastern Washington, and the box camera photographs show all the kids lined up on an old white horse—another girl now, and another boy would be born soon. There's one of Dad in those hated knee pants with Charlie in the background, his hair—like my own—already an early white beneath the hat that tips over one eye. Then they left the two-story frame house in the photograph and came back home. Charlie had been doing all the work, his children would tell me later. The brother agreed to sell Charlie's livestock and send him the money, but each of the animals met with ill luck and the money never arrived.

Today I can drive from this eastern Washington wheat country to Orofino in less than half a day on the winding two-lane roads. Dad described a much longer journey, with the whole family piling out to walk up the hills beside the Model T loaded with all their possessions. "And Bud's little banty rooster in a box tied to the running board," Auntie Grace would add. What Dad remembered about coming home to the ranch was the ring where a tepee had stood. Grace saw how a neighbor had opened the door so the cattle he had turned in to pasture here could use the log house as a barn. At eight, she was old enough to watch her mother's shoulders and know what it meant. "Dad built us a campfire and made biscuits in the old reflector oven," Grace told me. "We poured molasses over them. I never tasted anything so good in my life."

38    They were back. But there would be journeys closer to home. Grace and her sister Marie would run down the trail to the lower bench in the pitch-black night, as scared of what was out there in the dark as what was happening back in the house, where their older sister Mildred was dying. They were on their way to their grandparents' house where maybe they could crank the old wall telephone hard enough to bring the doctor up the hill—though they would learn later that the operator

had gone to sleep. Nothing would stop this: Alice's first child, who at sixteen had been doing housework for a woman they didn't realize was a typhoid carrier, was gone. People came this time, Aunt Grace would tell us later, not for Charlie's fiddle music or Alice's helping hands but to bring food and human voices to help muffle the sound of Charlie's hammer on the pine coffin boards. Edith, Dad's younger sister, remembered the walk to the cemetery to put wild flowers on the grave. A mile was a long way for her four-year-old legs. They went every day.

My father was nine when Mildred died. He didn't like to talk about it. "She had always mothered him," Mom told us. Watching Alice leave for the cemetery every day, or trotting along beside her trying to keep up, her children must have sensed that she would never quite return from this landscape of grief.

My mother was born on the Camas Prairie just above the Clearwater River, but her family had moved to Washington when she was a child, and then to Oregon, her father finding jobs in the barber shops as he followed his own parents' migrations through the Northwest. Our Tull uncles and aunts were scattered from Houston to Bremerton. They came to see us almost every year, though, as if they too were drawn home to the ranch.

But why didn't they have a place? A center of their own? I could tell there was another story, one no one would tell. It murmured like a winter creek below the ice.

A few summers ago I watched them, the four who had survived, gathered in a picnic circle again at the ranch. In their seventies now, and it was the first time I'd heard them touch the edges of the story. From my lawn chair I felt the swirl of voices, sudden anger stirring the summer air.

"Doesn't bother me," one uncle said. "Never think about it." Then he walked over to the fence and stared out past the barn.

The story was about their mother, Emily. She had grown up in Prince Edward Island, that place with "mackerel skies." Her mother taught her to play hymns on the piano and told her stories about

39

Highland Scots. School gave her the magic of words. And then one day a classmate told her the truth. She came home from sixth grade, climbed the stairs to the attic, and opened the trunk. In her father's Bible were the names of all his children, and hers was not among them. These were not her parents but her grandparents.

It was an old story. Emily's mother Mary was only a girl when she had gone to Boston to learn the millinery trade. The father (also a student; later a teacher at M.I.T.) was an Island boy too. When baby Emily was nine months old—with a birth certificate that labeled her "illegitimate"—Mary took the train to Idaho. Two aunts were already there. A clean slate, a place to begin her life again.

I see Mary through the sudden tears of Emily's four gray-haired children standing in the summer afternoon, their voices trembling. What kind of woman was she? The week she married, Mary fed ground glass to the pummeling dogs her husband loved; she had watched him tossing out his butcher shop scraps to feed them every night. Then they ran a boarding house in Pierce, the rough-and-tumble high timber town above Orofino where the gold rush had begun. No room for weakness here. Later, she would build a hotel in Peck, just down river. This business she would operate herself—her husband had died while on a journey to try to rescue their fifteen-year-old daughter, who had run off to hide along the Salmon River with a forty-year-old gunman, while Mary was home giving birth to their youngest child.

Last summer I asked my mother to show me Mary's house, which still dominates the skyline in the little town of Peck—only a dozen miles from Orofino, yet I had never seen it. Two stories, balconies all around, grounds spreading for a city block. Even a carriage house. I stopped the car at each side of the house, trying for the angle that would let me admire something about this woman—her tenacity, her toughness in the face of crippling social codes for women. Something besides that grinding glass.

When Emily arrived from Prince Edward Island—she had crossed the continent on the train with her grandmother sitting beside her— she was sixteen. "This is not my daughter," Mary said. And though a fragment of story says Emily's grandmother stayed on for a year while Emily went to work washing dishes in the boarding house, the Mary in our family story refused to be our mother.

40

Emily wanted to go to nursing school in Lewiston, and Mary would send all her other children to college. But she needed someone to help run the hotel. "I'll make it up to you," she said. Even before her marriage Emily was struggling with what the doctors would call melancholia. After she and Leonard had moved away she had a photograph made of her beautiful little girls to send Mary. (Look, Mother ...) During the good times, she loved to laugh, she always made friends with the neighbors, she told such stories. And wrote them, too, I would learn much later. I have her sixth-grade reader, pages crumbling with pressed violets and directives for "distinct utterance," Evangeline and Intimations of Immortality and Robert Burns and Emerson's "Compensation." She must have brought it with her on the train. On the back cover is this verse, copied in pencil:

> *When mountains and streams divide us*
> *And your face no more I see*
> *Take up your pen or pencil*
> *And write a line to me.*
> *We get back as much as we measure*
> *We cannot do wrong and feel right*
> *Nor can we give pain and feel pleasure*
> *For justice avenges each slight.*

When my own mother was twelve—by this time Emily had given birth to seven children, six of them surviving—the family left the little town in Oregon where Mom had climbed the green hills and played in the creek and swapped Gene Stratton Porter and Zane Gray library books with her sister, and returned to Idaho. It was early September 1929. The happy period of my mother's childhood was over. No more picnics at the baseball games, car horns honking *aoooga!* at the home runs. Melancholia had returned. Leonard lost his job in the barber shop. It was desperation, Mom says, that drove her folks to write Mary asking to borrow money to come home.

The woods were shutting down, and the loggers had no money in their pockets for haircuts. But the family was returning to a logging town too, and they were leaving behind Leonard's family to do it. When I was a child hearing this story, it seemed only right that Mom

41

would return to the Clearwater. Home. But I knew even then that Emily must have been desperate for more than food and shelter.

And Mary did send money—sixty-five dollars, which paid for a used Dodge cloth-top open car, "the kind you see in gangster movies," Mom described it. Leonard and the kids picked Oregon blackberries for weeks, selling them every night to the cannery truck from Eugene. Money for food and gas.

I try to picture the two-wheeled trailer they pulled behind them, filled with Emily's treadle sewing machine and Leonard's guitar, bedding and kettles and clothes. A family of eight. They spent the first night in Salem with Leonard's family. It was the last time he would see his mother. "But Daddy always made things seem like an adventure," Mom says. And it must have been an adventure, that trip up the Columbia Gorge on a road carved into rock walls, past the Vista House and the huge waterfalls, Bridal Veil and Horsetail and Multnomah. That night their beds were quilts laid on the floor of a tourist cabin: a two-room bare-wood shack with one bed, a wood cookstove, and a table. The next morning they passed Celilo Falls, where Indian men were fishing from platforms built out over the white water. And then the tires started to blow. They were in the eastern end of the gorge by now, the hot rocky canyon on a September afternoon. The kids carried water up from the river in their mother's big bread-making pan to test the tubes for leaks, and to splash on their faces. They were driving on at least one rim when a trucker stopped to help them. He could take the oldest kids with him as far as the next town, he said Leonard would follow in the lightened car and buy a better tire in Arlington. The trucker was a Mormon, he told the girls. Mom and Annie sat rigid on the truck seat, sure of what they'd learned from *Riders of the Purple Sage* about Mormons and villainy. While they waited for their parents in Arlington he bought the girls pie, but Annie was too frightened to eat hers.

Back on the road, they made better time where the road left the river at Wallula Junction to go through the Walla Walla farm country. Leonard showed the kids the house where he'd been born, by the little creek in Dixie. They were coming through the draws so much faster than his own parents had made the trip on their migration in a wagon with three little boys; his mother had soothed the baby's sunburn with her breast milk, all she had. He must have been trying not to think about Mary and what lay ahead.

There was no highway up the Clearwater in 1929; they had to climb the switchbacks of the Winchester grade to the Camas Prairie and descend again into Peck. It had rained and the road was deep with prairie mud. The car mired up to its axle. By now it was late evening of a long day's journey.

Amazingly, though, when Leonard hiked to the nearest farmhouse to ask for help, they turned out to be family—his cousin, another woman named Grace. Her husband harnessed his team and pulled the car out of the mud while Grace put a big pan of fried potatoes on the stove. It was a story Mom would tell over and over again—sleeping on the floor, full and warm and welcome.

But when they had crossed the prairie and wound down the old Melrose grade to Grandmother Mary's house in Peck the feeling of welcome was gone. The house itself amazed them, of course. Mary had bought it from the banker after retiring from the hotel, and the rooms were filled with his massive furniture. The whole block—garden, carriage house, and lawn—was enclosed by a hedge. It must have felt like a story from one of the library books. Emily's children would stand in the big dining room and hear the announcement that they were to call this woman "Aunt Mary." She had just paid sixty-five dollars for a "transformation"—a wig—and she didn't want a bunch of kids running around calling her Grandma. There would be the fresh Idaho tomatoes at dinner beside that elegant mirrored sideboard, and even a glimmer of hope when Uncle Willie returned from his work at his mother's general store, glad to see Emily and friendly to her children.

After supper Leonard unloaded their few belongings in the now-vacant hotel. There were beds stored in the old dining room with its big jacketed heating stove, and in the kitchen was a huge wood cookstove. This is where they were to live until Leonard found work and they could move. He parked the car, then, behind the hotel where it would stay, "property of Aunt Mary." The next morning he took the train to Orofino to look for work, and the kids started school in Peck.

By the time the three oldest kids crossed the Clearwater and headed upriver on top of the truckload of their family belongings, it was late

43

fall. It must have been after October 29, although to this family the Depression had long since begun. The leaves were gone and it was cold, the gray sky darkening in the canyon. Where was the green, and the soft-misted air they had left behind? That evening they were playing baseball in the area between the house and the street when it began to rain. "All the kids ran for cover," my mother writes, "except the Tull kids, who stood in the rain and were baptized into Idaho."

And now Emily emerges briefly from the shadows of this journey. They were walking down the sidewalk, Emily and the twelve-year-old girl who would grow up to be my mother, when a woman emerged from the barber shop where Leonard had found a job; Emily made a fist and planted it on the woman's jaw. Was it melancholia or ordinary human jealousy that made my grandmother break all the rules of social decorum? "I wanted the sidewalk to swallow me," says Mom. Of course. But something in me wants to cheer, raise my own fist in the air.

She was gone before I was born, so I never got to ask my grandmother if she found what she was fighting for. Maybe it was there, winter afternoons when she and her girls took turns with the ironing, reading aloud. Or that year they lived by the river on the Indian-owned land and her neighbor was a Nez Perce woman who became the kind of good friend she could talk with. Wild flowers grew along the river and the kids learned to swim across the current. As strange as it seems, she might even have found it when they were moving around Orofino's cheapest rentals—and living in a tent by the bridge the spring it flooded so badly. One day when their shelter was the little county house, the one with no running water and a toilet next door on the back porch of the landlord's house, Dr. Hopkins stopped his car as she walked back across the Orofino Creek bridge with her bucket of water to tell her, "Don't you let it get your goat, Emily." Sometimes a moment like that, just knowing someone sees you on the earth, can make the teetering world balance.

We understand depression better than we used to, and the hospital on the hill above the town can usually offer treatment that makes people feel better, not worse. Even now, though, not everyone makes it. Emily's children, who never quit mourning for the woman who slipped from the bridge into the Clearwater on a bitter January day thirteen years after they had returned to Idaho, continue to love this river. They live along its banks and seek the caress of its summer eddies. "Smell that river!" they say, rolling down the car windows. The clear current flows on into the Snake and the Columbia and at last the Pacific and then it curls back upon itself, something we can almost touch but not quite, a shaggy gray ghost heading home again.

# Letting the Women Talk

Late in the summer that my father died, my mother and I sat on the bank of the Clearwater River talking. The river was full of voices the way it is when the water is low. It would be the last year of a seven-year drought. Across the river a narrow ledge of flat land seemed just wide enough for the railroad track before the canyon wall started climbing again, but Mom was telling me about the two houses that used to be there. "That was where we lived the year I was a freshman, the year I got to go back to school," she said. I remembered how she and her brothers had walked down the railroad tracks and through the tunnel to town, how the buttercups grew along the banks in December that year. She had been wearing the blue coat, the one she would tear crawling through a barbed wire fence, "horsing around with Edie," and carrying the precious school books. This was a good year for her mother, too; Emily was in charge of the money Leonard sent home from Moscow—he had found a WPA job eighty miles away—and had her Nez Perce friend Mrs. Powatkee right next door. This small section of land along the river was still part of the reservation. Emily had someone to talk to.

We were talking too. We had always talked, from the time I first grudgingly admitted to myself that I would grow up to be a woman after all. In 1957, this was a prospect I needed help with. Every afternoon I carried my own books down the driveway, the dust from the school bus settling on my shoulders like October gnats, and when I came in the kitchen door my mother's eyes were waiting. She wanted to hear what had happened, and I wanted to tell her. Our voices wove a web I could cling to just above the mysteries and fears of junior high, and then I could change out of my school clothes and head out to the barn.

And Mom talked to me too. She apologizes, now. But if she hadn't talked to someone—we both know this—she would have imploded. Like so many women in the rural West, she had no one else to talk to but her children.

Letting the women talk can be dangerous.

We were sitting in the shade of the scrub pines where the Riverside Mill used to be. The current pushed over the riffles. Above our heads, a chickadee, then a flycatcher. Somewhere a pine beetle. "It was a good time," Mom said, looking across the river. She could almost see the houses, I knew. Smelling the river, she could hear her mother singing the old Harry Lauder songs. *It's a bra bricht moonlit nicht.* "I used to think that the reason the folks never had any money was that they didn't know how to manage it," she said. "But Mama did, I realize now. That winter Daddy sent home ten dollars a month, and she paid the rent, bought groceries … the Corner Store would deliver up the river if you bought a dollar fifty's worth." Mom was thinking about what had made living in that house such a good time. School. She even loved the walk down the tracks. It was an open winter, no deep snow to make her trip over the ties, and the hoboes who camped by the river looked down at their tin can buckets as she passed. Everyone, in their view of things, had a right to walk through the world.

"I had a bedroom in that little house," she said. "The only time I had a room of my own." I watched the vine maple shadow brushing her cheek and forehead. The beetle was silent now as she kept talking, her words spilling like the riffles below us. Now she was telling me about the year before they had lived in the house I could almost see across the river from us. That other year when she should have been a high school freshman but wasn't—because her father thought girls didn't need to go to school. Eighth grade was enough.

Like my mother, I had learned long ago to silence my rage at this part of the story. After all, we both knew, her father had had to quit school at nine himself to work on the farm. Eight grades was the goal; the fortunate kids graduated from eighth grade, and that was Lord's plenty. His daughters finished their first eight years of school just as the Depression was setting its teeth, ready to hang on to the chunk of your life it had bitten into. To go to high school you had to have enough money to buy books. Shoes, a coat. Paper.

But I felt rage, and so did my mother, I knew. Her younger brothers were still in elementary school, but there was no question that when the time came they would go to high school, somehow. Boys needed an education, Leonard said; girls didn't. When a classmate's father offered to buy textbooks for her—even when a young couple offered to let her work for her room and board while she went to high school—Leonard said no. No charity.

The year before they had moved to this house on the Indian land, Mom was telling me now, she didn't have a room to go to, or even a bed. "I slept on the couch. It wasn't long enough to stretch out, and the springs had broken so there was a deep hole in the middle," she said. "I hurt all night. It felt like there was no space for me in the world. Of course I helped Mama, but really there was nothing to do, nobody my age to talk to. The only bright spot was that new friend I made, the woman who lived next door." This young neighbor was older—twenty-six. But Beulah's family had lived far up the North Fork so at first she didn't get to go to school either; and although she had finally found a place to board in town and finished high school, she knew how my mother felt. In the evenings after Beulah got home from her job at the dime store they talked together, woman talk. "She was showing me how to knit," Mom said. One wonderful weekend Beulah invited her to the family home up the North Fork. They rode in an open car, wrapped in quilts. "It was colder than blazes!" Mom laughed. "But so much fun. I was supposed to sleep with Aunt Sally on what they called a sanitary cot, and when I got in the whole thing turned upside down with Aunt Sally in it. But she was nice about it. The next morning another uncle who slept in the main house—they lived right by the river, it was so beautiful—came over for breakfast. Sourdough biscuits and venison steak. The first time I'd had either." She stopped. "It was a big event." Then she was silent. I knew the rest of the story. There was nothing besides Beulah's friendship to help pull her up from her painful sleep into each morning. And her father had come home for a weekend visit and forbade her to be friends because Beulah's mother was living with a man she wasn't married to.

48

"He was judgmental," Mom said, looking across the river. "Sanctimonious. It was such a hard year for me. He didn't have to do that." Her voice shook. "He wasn't so perfect himself. He was a good man, but he wasn't perfect." We both knew what she was talking about.

I listened to the river, the drone of a small plane overhead. Mom turned to look at me. "I'm almost seventy years old," she said, "and it's the first time I've realized that I'm mad at my father."

I could be making too much of it. In a landscape like this, these canyons and benchlands topping out in high ridges—or in any landscape in the rural West, for that matter, the flatland sage country, the endless prairies of Ole Rolvag fame, the miles-wide high-desert cattle ranches—wasn't everybody isolated? You were pretty far from your neighbors. Claiming your section of the earth with stakes and barbed wire, squinting through a sextant as if you could really see the straight lines on a grid, must have encouraged you to "prove up" by building not only a cabin and a barn but a stout wall of Rugged Individualism around yourself. Alexis de Tocqueville, examining our culture's experiment in independence, saw the dangers long ago. These American *individuals*, he wrote, "owe nothing to any man, they expect nothing from any man; they acquire the habit of always considering themselves as standing alone, and they are apt to imagine that their whole destiny is in their hands." It's an attitude, he said, that not only makes "every man forget his ancestors, but it hides his descendants and separates his contemporaries from him; it throws him back forever upon himself alone and threatens in the end to confine him entirely within the solitude of his own heart."

In my family, though, and the families of people I could see around me as I was growing up, there was a special kind of separation reserved for women. The isolation was related to the land we lived on—not just the geography of the bridgeless canyons between our houses, but another kind of distance. I could hear it in the language. Old-growth forest is the term we use today, but then it was "virgin timber" waiting to be cut. Harvested, we say now. Managed. Or raped, depending on what the aerial photos reveal. "He plowed her, and she cropped," we read in school. I heard the elbow-in-the-ribs tone, but something else too. The rules and rings and fences to control girls and women, I could tell, had something to do with fear. If women got together too often they might grow, change, take on the characteristics of the earth in

49

spring, a creek in March, a seedling pine split at the stem, each half reaching for light and air. And then what?

But my mother would graduate from high school, as valedictorian, in 1937. She got to go back to school because of someone's mistake. A fluke, she calls it. A farmer's wife from the little prairie town called Cameron wanted Mom's older sister Annie to help with the wheat harvest cooking. The woman didn't know that Annie was already working for a young teacher's family in nearby Peck. So Mom got to go. "It wasn't easy," she laughs when she tells this story. "I was supposed to ride from Peck up to Kendrick on the train, but Annie's teacher wanted to take his family for a drive, so he took my train ticket money to pay for gas. Then he couldn't get his car started so we were late, and the farmer had gone to Kendrick to meet the train. I got off to a bad start." So much was riding on this job, a job she didn't even know how to do. "I burned the corn, drying it in the bottom of the oven. And I ruined the whipped cream cake by adding more cream—I'd never cooked with cream before, of course, and I thought if a little was good more would be even better. Finally a neighbor girl came to work with us, and she knew what to do and could show me." Breakfast, sandwiches at midmorning in the field, a big dinner, afternoon sandwiches, supper. She worked for twenty-two days and made eleven dollars. Enough to buy her books, the beloved blue coat. Shoes: a dollar fifty cents. Two dresses. She could start school that fall.

The next summer she worked at the hospital as a tray girl, pulling the thick-crockery meal trays six at a time up the dumbwaiter. Long after this job was over, her body would wear the history of that weight. There were no days off. On the fourth of July she paid another girl her whole day's pay, fifty cents, to work just the evening hours of her shift while she went on a picnic up the river with her best friend Lola and Lola's sister and brother, a handsome boy she had a crush on. But at the end of the summer she would have forty-five dollars, enough for clothes and books and paper and even fifteen dollars to get her teeth fixed. By this time she was also working for Dr. Hopkins—she didn't know for sure, but thought maybe Hopkins had arranged the hospital job for her—after school, Saturdays, and Sunday mornings. She cleaned house, mostly, though for a while Mrs. Hopkins made her wear a little maid's apron and hat and serve her dinner guests. (*How did you stand it?... I always knew I was just as smart as they were.*) The best part was when the Hopkins family was on vacation and she got to clean the books—slowly, turning pages. "It took me two weeks to clean that bookcase!" Such riches. And they paid her fifteen dollars a month. Then she moved in, sharing a bedroom with the nine-year-old daughter. "They were sort of making me part of the family," she said, and now the pay was eight dollars a week.

What would have happened if she had not met my father? Mrs. Hopkins gave her an ultimatum: quit dating him or quit working for her. "He had a *terrible* reputation," Mom says. None of the young lumberjacks who hit town on Saturday nights with their paychecks would have met with Mrs. Hopkins's approval. But my mother was a girl in love with this raven-haired boy who walked her around town in the dark singing "Winter Wonderland," snowflakes catching on his eyelashes. So she moved back home and got a job working for a woman who did mending and tailoring in the back of a store on Main Street near her father's barber shop. Twenty cents an hour. It wasn't enough, and now for the first time she would have to beg her father for a dime. She needed notebook paper. The handsome young man who was to become my father didn't want her scrubbing other women's floors. He'd pay for her school supplies, he said. He was working in the woods on one end of a crosscut saw, a small man but strong and driven and youthful enough to keep ahead of desperate out-of-work lawyers and college men in the pay-per-log system of the Depression lumber business. No, that wasn't right, Mom thought. "Let's get married," he said. "Then you can accept my money." It was March 1, a day of deep spring snow. Mom was eighteen. She would keep living with her parents until the end of the school year while her teachers raised their eyebrows and measured her waist with their gaze. She would graduate.

51

Only then did she learn that the Hopkinses had been planning to send her to college.

When I was a child growing up on the ranch above the Clearwater canyon, I knew in my bones that education was the answer. Not to poverty—Horatio Alger stories didn't touch me. But to sadness, loneliness. A book felt as good in my hand as my dog's head felt, pushing against my knee. Education wasn't just in books, though. It was in stars, too. And music. People's voices. And deer tracks, the red and yellow flashes on the blackbird's wing, the smell of Easter lilies behind the cabin. Veins in the crabapple leaves, frozen to the mud puddle in the driveway. Yeast pushing the bread up to the top of the pan. The smell of sulphur from the match head. It was Mom who showed me that it was everywhere. Educate: "to lead out," I would learn in Latin class. But I already knew that lesson. I can close my eyes and see her, all those mornings when I was still numb with sleep and pulling on overshoes and layers of wool to push out into the darkness and the smell of snow and barnyard. She is propped in a chair at the cluttered kitchen table in her ragged chenille robe, stealing a few minutes between getting Dad off to work at 5:30 and getting the kids up and ready to meet the school bus, the oatmeal kettle on the stove and ice box cookies still warm on the waxed paper sheet; peanut butter sandwiches, thermoses, ironed shirts, Dad's old coffee cup. She's reading the encyclopedia.

She's learning what she didn't get to learn in high school because she had to take the commercial classes. Shorthand, accounting, bookkeeping. After high school she would have to get a job. ("I didn't get to take chemistry!" she would tell us. "Or biology. You kids take the science courses, take all you can. And foreign language. History— take history.") But she wouldn't use her business courses after all. The summer after her graduation my father's eyes reacted to a chemical used to keep the pine lumber from bluing and he nearly lost his sight. For two years he couldn't work. They moved into the one-room log cabin he had built on his parents' ranch; he sold his old Model A and they rode to town standing in the back of his parents' truck with the younger kids. There was no money. None. But he didn't want her to go to work. How would it look, a man not being able to support his wife? His wife supporting *him*?

Besides, in this family, women didn't drive.

And so began another kind of isolation. They were six miles and almost 2500 feet above town. There were only her in-laws, Dad's parents and his brother and two of his sisters, and the first grandchildren. Mom helped one of those babies into the world: "Alice held one leg and I held the other," she told me. She was learning to cook. I grew up hearing the story of the pumpkin pie she made with mustard Alice had sent across the field in a spice can labeled GINGER. "I had eaten my way through two pieces and was on the third before she took her first bite," Dad always laughed. "You should have seen her face." I did see her face not long ago when she realized as we talked that Alice must have done this on purpose, that the whole point of the story wasn't her new-bride ignorance. I still have that old Rochdale Feed Store diary-calendar I found in the trunk when I was growing up. Just below my father's familiar scrawl, "Watch Cow," I recognized Mom's writing. "Lynches, Lynches, Lynches!"

There was, though, the community women's club—strangers she was getting to know. "Grammie talked me into hosting it once," Mom tells me. "I made a big pan of scalloped potatoes. It was all I had. Of course there wasn't enough room in the cabin. They sat on the bed, on the cedar chest … People were supposed to bring food. Only one woman did—a jar of pickled crabapples. Imagine."

But then came the quarrel which isolated her from even this gathering of women. All these years later we grandchildren struggle to understand it, what it was about and how it could have torn such a rift that even while we were growing up we didn't belong to our own community. It was Alice's quarrel with Lizzie Anderson, a woman her own age, the mother of the more prosperous family who lived on the ridgetop just above us. Something about money. The women had held bake sales and raised three hundred dollars, an amazing amount in the Depression, to improve the kitchen in the Grange hall. It was one of those disputes that we all get into from time to time, burning with passion over an issue that, two or three years later, no one will remember. Lizzie's opinion prevailed—save the money for a new Grange hall. Alice and her daughter walked home, furious. "I hadn't gone that day, for some reason," Mom tells us, so that's all she knows of the details.

Nothing they could do would heal this wound. The entire community withdrew from Alice's family. That fall when Mom and

Dad went to the potluck Thanksgiving dinner at the old schoolhouse, no one would speak to them. "We were snubbed," Mom says, still hurt. It doesn't make sense, even now. How could we have grown up in such communal silence—the same families still lived around us—over such a small thing? Or maybe not such a small thing, this question of how best to build community. It was a community Alice and Charlie had long been part of, though. People had always come to them for help; they had been there to raise the school and make music for the dances. And, as it turned out, the new Grange hall was never built. Didn't these women realize, I wonder, that difficult as it was to get along with Alice—she had never really recovered from the death of her oldest child, and her tongue could be sharp—it must have been even more challenging for her daughter-in-law?

Then came the years when we were the only Lynches on the place, my growing-up years. And then my father's own quarrel with his mother, and our enforced isolation not only from his sister Edith, Mom's close friend since high school, but from the world. That first summer we didn't leave the ranch even to go the six miles to town. Once a week Dad stopped on his way home from the mill to pick up a stack of books the librarian had chosen for us kids—whispered messages from other human beings—but for months my mother didn't talk to another female older than twelve.

Not long ago I sat in a hot springs pool just off the McKenzie River in Oregon with my friends Jane and Janet at the end of a week-long women's writing workshop called *The Flight of the Mind*. We were the same age and our mothers were too—seventy-nine, turning eighty that year. "I wish they could be here," we all said, practically in the same breath. We sank deeper into the steaming mineral water, letting ourselves float on the exhaustion of a week of truth-telling, sharing stories, talking. Listening. "I wish there had been something like this in their lives."

*My mother is lying on a hospital gurney. We're waiting for the technician to do an ultrasound. Her voice touches my face, brushes against my hair. "If I hadn't been married, I'd certainly have gone," she says. She had wanted to join the military*

*during World War II, I have just learned. More than fifty years later, she's telling me about it for the first time. "One married woman in town did go, in fact, after her three sons left. Her husband didn't want her to go, but she told someone later that it had saved her marriage. A girl from my class went, too." She pauses, trying to breathe slowly, deeply. Her heart has been racing. Then she laughs. "Maybe I'd have married a GI and raised my five kids in Levittown!"*

*I have never heard any of this story. She had wanted to buy an atlas, she says, to follow the war—she had only a vague idea of the borders in the news stories. Dad had said, "Yeah, that's exactly what we need!" We were so poor, she says. He wasn't the least bit interested—only interested in staying out of it as long as he could.*

*We are silent together. I'm holding her hand just below the purple bruise of the IV. "Women were pilots, mechanics, all sorts of things."*

*I don't know any words to give back; I want to smash things, yell, swear at the sterile ceiling. But I hold her hand in both of my own. Listening hard.*

It wasn't that my mother hated the ranch. She loved it. It fed her. The sunrise painting the yellow pines every morning, the morning star, rusty ninebark, and vine maple leaves, the pink and gold of sunset when Huckleberry Butte turned evening blue. Western bluebirds in the crabapple tree; wrens in the eaves. Violet-green swallows, baby blue-eyes fighting their way up through the alfalfa all summer long. But she had five children to feed, their shirts and dresses to sew, a two-acre garden and weeks of canning to do, diapers, bread to make, and the washing—at first on a scrub board, later with a wringer washer. Sprinkling, hours of ironing. No electricity and no running water; even after the Rural Electric Association and Reddy Kilowatt came into our lives when I was five and even after Dad piped in the water when I was eleven, there wasn't enough water for a bathroom. Keeping us all clean, just washing the dishes three times a day, was a back-aching effort. It ate up the hours. The radio—that Valentine's Day love gift—touched something that lived inside her, somewhere between her heart and her spine, and it held her up. KWSU Pullman. College lectures, Scheherezade, Peer Gynt. Singing in the kitchen.

After Monte had nearly died in his crib with his first asthma attack, though—it had taken such a long time to get the message to Dad at

55

the mill, and then for him to race up the hill to give them a ride back down to the hospital—Mom propped the little boys behind her elbow, started up the old red Dodge pickup and bounced around the alfalfa field until she was ready to pull out onto the one-lane grade with the logging trucks. It was 1958. She was forty years old.

A few years later, after the mastectomy and the radiation and a year of kneading five-loaf batches of bread to make her right arm work again—the boys were all in school by this time—she drove to town and got a job. For fifteen years she would work to help the Army Corps of Engineers who were damming the North Fork of the river she loved. "That job saved my life," she says. Together they built the third-highest concrete dam in the country.

When I visit my mother now, we lie in bed, talking into the night. She teaches me how to tell the stories that have been shamed into silence, but maybe even more importantly, how to listen to them. How do I hear Bessie's story, when the muffled words finally break through? Mom's Aunt Bessie was the family embarrassment, the fifteen-year-old who ran away with a man who had just shot his way out of jail (he had been locked up for cattle rustling, but the story hinted at much worse crimes) and hid out with him on the River of No Return, Idaho's rugged Salmon River country, raising their thirteen children by herself. This much I had heard before—and that when she finally contacted her mother, years later, "Aunt Mary" had asked her, "Why didn't you write?"

"At first I had Reid, and then I had the children," Bessie said.

I had thought it meant: how cold! (And, secretly: what poetic justice, this circle of rejection—a woman rejects her firstborn daughter, and then the girl she is willing to claim as her first child rejects her, and threatens all that hard-bought respectability.) Yes, my mother says. But listen again. *At first* I had Reid; *then*, I had the children. My eyes stare into darkness.

56

It was my mother who ended Dad's devastating family quarrel by reaching out to Alice, listening to her stories and writing them down. And now she is a member of a larger community, one not popular with all her neighbors in the Clearwater canyon country. She has joined the National Organization for Women, the Nature Conservancy, the Sierra Club. The thing she likes best about the classes at the local library—geology, writing workshops, book clubs—is that people aren't afraid to speak up. "It's not like when I worked for the Corps of Engineers and took those government workshops. People were so quiet, afraid to venture an opinion or ask a question " Recently she stopped in to visit her old friend Beulah. She hadn't seen her, she said, since Beulah's ninetieth birthday party.

Not long ago we stood on the bluff overlooking the Clearwater as a Nez Perce storyteller talked about the whirlpool below us. The river has changed, he told us. Even below a dam, a river is never the same, and the highway and railroad embankments have altered the current where it swings around this corner, too. The eddy isn't as fierce as it once was. Logs used to stand on end and disappear into it during the log drives that ended in the 1960s. It was a hundred feet deep. For thousands of years, people came here seeking visions. He stood silent for a moment, his eyes watching our faces. No one spoke. "It is still a place of power," he said.

I looked at my mother. Her face was glowing in the early April air; a chill breeze and sun. Highway travelers can stop to rest at this place above the river—there are green picnic tables under the pines now— and when I'm driving home I always pull in, climb down the bank and taste the Clearwater splashed on my face. The eddy calls me, and the whitewater riffles above it. Beyond the storyteller's shoulder the whirlpool was outlining itself in bark and wood chips, this spring's runoff. Can we learn to hear the spirits of this place? I wondered. Are we listening carefully enough? The women in my family seek out this place like pilgrims. We sit at the tables or under the small pines above the steep bank, talking. Sometimes we are on our way to visit my mother, seeking an elder's help to tell our most difficult stories. Above this river's place of power, we hear our voices pulling truths from their secret corners. We imagine possibilities. Maybe we can learn to celebrate our survival, forgive even ourselves. Often, by the time we reach my mother's house—cake and coffee and the sound of laughter, the look of light on a familiar face—all we need is the circle of her open arms.

57

# Water Stories

My father hated water.

He was afraid of it, my mother said. Because of the wreck. The car had rolled into the canyon, tumbling end over end; the dark current of the Salmon River waited at the bottom. Of course it wasn't water that had crushed his friend's chest and sent the other CCC boys to the hospital in Grangeville. Their car had landed on the boulders just above the river. ""But after that," Aunt Edie told us, "he was just never the same."

"Water is a medicine," I would hear the Indian elder Louie Dick say many years later. He had come to my classroom to try to explain. "Water enters and is the only thing that can touch the heart." *Listen,* I heard myself whispering. But my father was already gone.

In the shadows of the draws and under the steep, timbered hill that we called the upper forty were the old wells. The splintered boards that had covered them were gone now and all that remained were sunken holes, filled almost to the top with broken field rock. It was a mystery I couldn't fathom, this water in the earth. How could there be water— tiny rivers, invisible lakes—under the ground?

On the hottest days we could feel our red pump handle catch and the water coming up the pipe toward us even before it burst out to splash over our heads. It made my shoulder ache, carrying the buckets up the trail to the house. A dipperful tasted like I'd swallowed sky, cold all the way down.

In late August, when the well was low, Dad lifted the planks and lowered himself into the smell of waterslick earth. Cleaning the well meant bailing it out, letting it slowly refill while we rinsed our toothbrushes with stale "town water" from the zinc barrel and begged Mom for Kool-Aid. Something about that well descent made Dad yank at his bootlaces and pull the muddy shirt over his head, his eyes shut.

None of the dug wells last forever, they said, and ours was failing. I trailed my father around the Idaho benchland, watching his shoulders twist the auger, the curl of red clay crumbling between his fingers. How could a man who hated water find it? One evening Dad came home in the company of a water witch. "Put your hands right here," the man told me. "Some people can feel water, some can't." The limber willows twisted in my palms, pulled to the earth by something I couldn't touch. There was something there, below the grass.

My brothers and I followed our father's desperation across the summers that followed—making traps, I thought, for something to stumble into. Sometimes there was enough seepage at the bottom of our holes to make the shovels pull at our shoulders, muck that ripped the bottom out of the old metal tub. "The hell," said my brother Tom, and threw the first handful at me. We clambered out of the pit, mudslick and crazy, our aim wild, tasting the sweet insanity of laughter.

"There's always the Cartwright spring," our father announced one night over supper, following his decision to fill in another hole. "My Old Man traded for the water right on that spring, and it's still valid, it's registered in the courthouse."

But it wasn't on our land. It was on our neighbor's land, just past the corner of the upper hill, hidden in firs.

Besides, it would cost a lot to pipe it over, he said.

Other people along the bench and on the ridge above us were drilling deep, permanent wells. They paid by the foot, whether or not the driller hit water, as much as a car, the down payment on a tractor. As one summer turned into the next, we sat at the supper table and heard the reports: a vein as thick as a matchstick, thick as a pencil. Or we counted down with our neighbors: *in two thousand dollars and nothing yet. Can't afford to go deeper. Can't afford to stop.*

"Paying for a dry well," my father would say.

59

The month before I left for college I walked across the stubbled east field through a shower of grasshoppers while Martin Luther King stood on the steps of the Lincoln Memorial and sent his dream out to those upturned faces. Come September I sat in the auditorium for freshman orientation thinking: *everyone here had a shower this morning, all of us, like standing in the rain, like kids.*

❦

When Dad finally did drill a well—not that fall, but three dry summers later—they hit a small vein. Finally we could have a bathroom, with a shower, but we still had to ration water in the summer. And we couldn't water a garden or a lawn, or fruit trees.

Later that fall the old Cartwright place sold to an outsider and Dad decided to trade his right to that spring to his long-time neighbor, Jake: Dad's water right to the spring, now situated on some newcomer's land, for Jake's sixteen acres of hillside above the road next to our upper forty. It was a skyline both men wanted to keep. They liked to watch the sun hit those pines in the mornings before it rolled down the mountain to touch their families, side by side along the benchland. Jake wanted to be sure nobody cut the trees on that steep hill above his house. And he needed the water held deep inside the old spring. It was just across his fenceline.

But the man who had bought the land where the spring bubbled brought in a big Cat and dozed out a pond. The spring proved as powerful as Dad had promised: it filled a pond that looked, from the timbered ridge above Jake's house, more like a lake. We could see wooden structures—nesting platforms for geese, we guessed—and we heard a new sound. Bullfrogs.

"He says that water right you traded me was no good," Jake said.

"It's as good as my Old Man's word," said my father. "Go look in the courthouse."

"I looked," Jake said. He wanted his hillside back.

The newcomer was subdividing. Some of the houses were right behind Jake's fence line. We could hear people hammering, calling their children, hear their dogs barking. At night the summer-heavy chorus of bullfrogs troubled our dreams like penned cows bawling for their calves at weaning time.

"Jake should have fought for that water right. It was old, but it was a clear right," my father said. Now, of course, it was worthless to either family.

I wasn't sure. I remembered Dad's arm gesturing back over his shoulder toward the spring, those nights at the supper table. Maybe it was true, but not right. Can water really be owned? I wondered.

When my mother saw Jake's wife crossing the field, she put the coffee on and walked out through the corn rows to meet her, but the men had nothing left to say to each other. Finally my father died and Jake moved away.

Now, in Oregon, I watch the journey of the Umatilla. One summer I saw a pair of spring chinook digging a redd in a clear pool of this river's North Fork. Their bodies arched against the gravel and splashed bright half circles above the water. I stood in the August dust, watching.

The *East Oregonian* had carried stories about the water-use problems of the Umatilla River, the clash between irrigation and salmon, but I wasn't thinking about that. When words came to me again I thought, I've been waiting all my life to see this.

That summer, too, the *East Oregonian* offered this headline: "Police Say Man Tried to Kill Son: Water dispute boils over when shots allegedly fired." The man was eighty-one, his son fifty-two. "A longstanding dispute over a water right," the district attorney explained.

The story of the West, we're told, is the struggle for water. But I stared at the newsprint the way I had looked down into those jagged heaps of rock. For some reason I thought of the way ice floes climb the Umatilla's banks during the breakup, and the bridge-smashing roar of spring runoff. Then the cool deep green of mid-June, and the narrow current of August.

The people of the Umatilla define themselves by their river drainage; they belong to this river: these canyons and rolling fields. I am of the Clearwater drainage, from the benchland riding the ridge between Whiskey Creek and Orofino Creek. I grew up in the reflection of an old tinted photograph—the whitewater of Orofino Creek plunging around the mica-flecked granite on its way down. My mother skipped school to go on a picnic with my father and they took that picture. They were in love and taking risks; he stood on a rock above the raging water steadying the old box camera. "No, no," she tells me now. "I skipped with Aunt Edie, not with your dad. That seemed— wrong, you know. To skip with a boy."

Always, just when I think I understand, there is more. *Don't go in over your knees,* Dad had called to us when our ankles bent in the blue-green current of Bruce's Eddy. *It will pull you under.* Years later I watched my

61

own son, our little River Bear, his wet legs dark with sand on the roll and tumble down the dunes into the Columbia. When my parents came to visit, Dad followed us to the family swim at the city pool. His brown arms clung to the side of the pool, white legs blurring against the blue cement, as he grinned at my son's water-splashed voice: "Look, Grandad! Watch this!" I had not known Dad owned a pair of swimming trunks.

Downstream from here, the Umatilla joins the waters from the Clearwater in the Columbia. A few years ago I met a woman whose father grew up on the big island just below the Columbia's Celilo Falls. On March 9, 1957, this man had stood with his children on the gray basalt ridge overlooking Celilo Falls and watched the waters behind the newly built Dalles Dam erase the whitewater and silence the petroglyphs. They saw the big island, their summer home, become a shadow. Then the family had turned south, heading for the dry juniper promise of Warm Springs.

When she tells me this story, I am sitting at her table in the house beside the Deschutes River—a house made from sections of a nearby Japanese Internment Camp barracks her father skidded in and nailed together. Her table is long; there is room on these benches, she says, for everyone. The meal we are about to eat will begin and end with water. Water bears us, feeds us, heals us. I think of my father, his struggle, finally, just to breathe. At the end, he knew, his kidneys would fail. "I won't do it," he had told us. Drown, he meant. "Chuus." Our cups hold the taste of sky.

# Guns

## 1

They look so innocent. They must have hired a photographer, or maybe one came by on a Sunday afternoon when Alice's folks from the lower bench were visiting, hauling a camera and tripod out of his wagon and catching them in just the right mood to pose for one of those postcard photos. They're lined up in front of the old log house, with Great-Grandma and Grandpa Scoles white-haired in the doorway. It's hard to imagine my grandmother Alice this young—mid twenties?—and smirking like that, like a kid herself. And Charlie is posing, one hand on his hip, his mouth only pretending to be serious. It's a kind of joke. A parody: the family in the American West. Charlie braces the .30-40 Krag on the earth in front of him. Mildred, the oldest of his and Alice's children, reaches just to her father's elbow, and the pistol she wears in a holster hangs to her knee. Marie holds the familiar little single-shot .22 rifle. They scowl fiercely at the camera. Gracie wears a two-year-old's pout as she dangles what looks like a top-break Smith and Wesson .44, and Alice, dressed in white, holds out the shotgun, the 12 gauge "Long Tom" with Damascus barrels, so tall it reaches almost to her shoulder. And there's Dad, propped in the baby carriage, holding the Saturday Night Special of his childhood's era, a little Bulldog .41 rimfire pistol about the size of a baby rattle. His small head is bent over it, fascinated.

I found this picture on a rainy afternoon when I was eleven. When it slid from between the cardboard-framed portraits of all those stern black-and-white strangers that my parents kept stacked in Uncle Joe's old army footlocker, I couldn't put it down. I knew this much about guns: they weren't toys. Yet here they were, my elders, playing. How did it feel to be one of those kids, holding those real guns? Especially that big pistol. And that was another thing. I'd not yet heard the word "handgun," but I knew my dad didn't have much use for them. The West wasn't as wild as the movies would have us believe, he said. People didn't really wear holsters strapped to their legs.

So what was my grandfather doing with three pistols?

And if Marie could hold the .22, why couldn't I?

It hung on the wall of the house I grew up in, just below the deer rifle, Dad's Winchester .32 . I could not imagine shooting the .32. It could break your shoulder, I thought. Only my father was strong enough not to be knocked over just by the sound. But the .22 was small, a boy-sized gun. The little rifle glowed in the stories he told around our kitchen table after breakfast on long winter mornings. "The Old Man gave me that .22 for my birthday when I was eight," he said. "And one box of shells. 'I'll give you a penny for every squirrel tail,' he told me. The next box of shells would cost forty-nine cents. There were fifty shells."

How could it surprise me that my father was perfect? I had never seen him miss. The .22 was real, too, sized for a boy's reach but in the right hands even a hunting gun. Once, a few months after his eighth birthday, he'd had to walk home, carrying his little rifle, to ask for help. He was still too small to drag the deer across the snowy east field. It had leaped across the road ahead of him and he had shot it between the eyes. "After that," he laughed, "the Old Man took away my shells and gave them out two or three at a time. I had to bring in a squirrel tail for each one, too."

I was almost a boy. "Bette's my boy," he had said when I was three, traipsing after him to the barn, and that was when I knew that if I tried hard enough to be a boy I could be real, or almost real. But in our house guns were only for Dad. And no BB guns. "Guns aren't toys," he said. *Always think about what's behind your target*, he told us. *A gun is always loaded. Never, never let the barrel point at a person.* It was as if someday we would be trustworthy ourselves, ready to be given a rifle for our eighth birthdays even though those had long passed. Then, the summer I was nine, he took my brother Tom over on the hill and held him while he shot the .22. Tommy was four. I was *nine*.

When I was twelve, I took my father's single-shot .22 down from the nails he had pounded into the wall and taught myself to shoot. There weren't many shells: less than two dozen. I had found them in his dresser drawer, the small box of space he reserved for his things, the cast iron bulldog bank, the leather strap. I was breaking all his rules at once.

64

I remember the quiet house, hot July sun making the dust dance over by the window. And the walk through the east field stubble, how light the little rifle felt, how it hung in my hand. How easy it was, really, after all. Just past the corner of the field, across the barbed wire fence, lay a stash of discarded whiskey bottles, their long necks catching the sun. In the shadow of the timbered hill rising above our field, people pulled their cars off the road to drink. My friend Mike propped the whiskey bottles on the fenceposts—the broken glass will fall right under the fence, he said, and there's no stock here anyway—and I put the sight in the groove. The neck shattered like stars, afternoon fireworks. When Mike took a turn one of the old shells exploded, slivers of lead curling backward to blacken his cheek, but it was nothing, he said. We rationed the bottles, three explosions each: neck, middle, bottom. It was magic, it was Dad's story all over again. We never missed.

I didn't want to shoot squirrels, though. I just wanted to shoot. Mike said that was dumb; you had to shoot something, he said, something that moves. It's a lot harder. Sure enough, he missed. But when I aimed at a running squirrel it stopped running, lay there on the earth, its throat neatly sliced. Mike's awe was angry. "How'd you *do* that?" he asked, but I couldn't talk. His foot reached toward the squirrel, then drew back. His BB gun looked like one of my little brothers' toys as he dragged the butt along the trail up to the road. He was going home.

Mom and the kids were in the kitchen when I got back to the house, and I didn't try to hide the rifle. There was no hiding this—the world was a different place, I was a different person.

It took a long time, a week. Finally Dad noticed the missing shells, or maybe Mom said something. "Well, I got another box of shells," he said. "Be sure to leave a few—we need to keep some on hand." He was grinning.

But of course it wasn't that easy; nothing about guns is easy. The boys who were twelve the summer I learned to shoot would come home from the war complaining about the guns. "They gave us bad guns," they said. "The guns didn't work." At night their breath would push out of their chests like powder, and the small muscles in their hands kept shooting. I would watch the powder-white explosions of Sheetrock in my own house, patch the punctured hole in the blue quilt. We had to replace the shrapnel-jagged sink. And once I stood outside the bedroom door, knowing I should go in and wrestle the gun away, or try to. Alcohol had given the visions bodies, flesh and smells and black sounds from the sky. Who was this man I had followed down the hall? Could this be the man I had married? The same man who sang with his head tipped back, the one whose body curved around my own all night, turning together as if we were one person? I put my hand on the doorknob. *Dean wouldn't shoot me.* Then I let go and stepped back around the corner, waiting for the sound.

Yet that spring, when I would send away this man I loved and try to learn to live without him, Dad went back into his bedroom and came out with the little .22 rifle. "I want Josh to have it," he said. "And I may not be around next year." For his grandson's eighth birthday, he meant. His emphysema was getting worse.

In this generation's photograph—the one I developed in my darkroom, seeking peace in its black silence—Dad's arms circle my son's small shoulders like a blanket. He is guiding his hands, teaching him to shoot.

"I understand that people disagree about guns," one of my college students said to me recently. "But how can *anybody* justify giving a gun to a child?" She was thinking about that little boy in camouflage in the *Newsweek* photograph. And all those pictures burned into all our brains.

By the time my father bought the .38 the perfect legends of my childhood had begun to disintegrate, dissolving from the center outward. The accidents had already begun. First in my own house: the bullet traveling the length of the little trailer we were living in then, through the bathroom, over the center of Josh's bunk bed, into the bear on the small carved totem pole just behind my head. I was washing dishes at the kitchen sink; Josh was on the couch. His legs were still so small that his feet stuck out past the edge of the green and brown plaid. He was looking at Mr. Rogers on the little black-and-white screen next to the splintered hole in the bookcase. On both ends of the house, his parents screamed: "Are you there? Are you there?"

And then breathing again, and smoke.

There were bullet holes in other family members' walls, too. Even a sawed-off shotgun stashed behind a pickup seat, a bedside handgun aimed at the soft footsteps of approaching cats, derringers stored in hip pockets, just in case. When one of them fired, the bullet lodged just behind my brother's right knee. Even Dad shot a small hole through his own window, he admitted with a grin. And he had a concealed weapons permit.

He had changed his mind about handguns. At first it was a .22 pistol—something he'd always wanted, he said. Just to plunk at cans with. "Well, Bud, what are you waiting for?" said a man in the sports shop where Dad had stopped to buy his fishing license. Just some guy standing around, someone whose name I don't even remember. And then, just after the doctors had told him that oxygen tanks were in his future, he bought the .38, the Saturday Night Special. "He wants to be able to protect me," Mom said. "He feels so helpless now that he can't catch his breath. How can I take that away from him?" It was a question none of us could answer.

The hard truth is, Dad had been leaning toward suicide for a long time—long before he first looped the oxygen tubes around his ears. One August afternoon when I was seventeen I helped my mother look for him. He had taken the rifle and disappeared, and we both knew what we were looking for. When he finally came home, he said he'd gone for a walk, that's all—taken the .32 along because he'd seen signs of a black bear. I remember how it felt to call his name into the hot air—my hair still damp from the river; he and Mom had quarreled when she insisted on letting us swim in the North Fork at a community picnic—and I remember his sheepish half-grin when I saw him coming back through the east field. So I wasn't surprised when, the next time he took the rifle down into the woods, there was no mistaking his intentions. I was away in graduate school by this time, but Mom saw a letter from me sticking out of his shirt pocket when she followed him into the trees to stop him, and it felt as if I were still there, calling his name.

Ten years later, when emphysema tightened his chest and he promised to end it before it got too bad, I tried to think, *this is different.* For the first few years I just listened, my stomach clenching. Near the end, though, I was begging him, casting my words into the same kind of hot afternoon silence as when I was seventeen. *Please, Dad. If you can, try to hang on.* For two years, three? I had lain awake every time I visited, listening for the shot; I knew he wanted me there to help Mom survive his death when it came. His would be her third suicide: her mother, and then a few years ago, her oldest brother ... Of course he had told all of us, all his children, but I was the one who lived closest. By the end he was telling everyone. His sisters, the nurses, even the chaplain at his last hospital stay. Everyone, of course, except Mom. If he didn't have a gun, he'd use a knife, he said, making slashing motions at the inside of his elbows. Something sure. Overdosing on the pain pills might not do it. Might just make him a vegetable.

It wasn't the pain he could not bear; it was the thought of suffocating as his lungs filled with fluid. But his hands were so weak that the only gun whose trigger he could still pull was that small pistol, and he had promised Mom that he wouldn't use it. "I've never broken a promise to your mother, and I don't intend to start now," he told me. Then, two mornings later, he did.

She was sleeping on the couch just outside his little sickroom. What woke her was the silence. He had turned off the oxygen machine. And then that flat-handed slap. Such a small sound, really. When I heard it from her bedroom, where I was spending the night, I thought *something has fallen.*

# 2

Before I took the .22 down from the wall and taught myself to shoot, guns were only for Dad—even the day Tom got to shoot, it was really Dad's arms circling Tom's, the father who was wise and strong, incapable of a wrong shot. Josh still has that .22. For years I kept it for him in my own closet. He and his now-sober father like to drive out into the country and shoot at targets; sometimes they go pheasant hunting together. I wish that, like so many people who didn't grow up with guns, I didn't understand this. But I do.

I had watched my father using his rifle to feed us—hunting, and butchering the animals we raised, their deaths instant and painless. I watched him quickly end the suffering of an injured steer, and I took in the message of my community: be prepared, be responsible. Be humane. I'd heard the tears in my neighbors' voices when the blue buckskin colt got caught in the barbed wire and they didn't have the .30-.30 in the truck, they always had it but not that day ... and once, when my own headlights pierced a thrashing coyote with a broken back in the middle of a lonely highway, I felt the same guilt: *I don't even have a gun.*

Nearly all rural people have this intimate knowledge of guns. We know that our neighbors, if not our selves, carry guns along in their lives the way other people carry flashlights or road maps, spare change for the toll booth.

But even this knowledge can become a painful burden. That night in my writing workshop cabin, most of the women were city people. When we asked the camp caretaker to come help us shoo a woodrat out of the bathroom—someone had left a banana peel in the wastebasket—I had pictured him coming up the trail with a broom, something to help us direct the little furry animal toward an exit so we wouldn't step on it during the night. But the Fishtrap workshop was held in my corner of Oregon, just outside the town of Joseph where I had lived for over a decade. So I'm the one who should have known he'd bring a gun.

Yet I couldn't get past my own denial. A pistol? He wouldn't shoot a pistol inside the cabin. He raises llamas, he cooks for us, his grandchildren visit ... he's not even drinking. My friend Lola tucked her feet into her sleeping bag and shot one-liners at him, frantic efforts at diversion, but my own tongue was frozen. None of the women had meant this to happen; none of them knew the words to stop it. *It must be a joke.* He tossed a cookie into the middle of the bathroom floor and waited, and when the woodrat scurried forward for more treasure, the gun went off.

There were no new holes in the cabin wall. He had used something called "snake shot," a .22-sized casing loaded with tiny seeds of lead. "Oh my God," someone said. I recognized the faces of the women who had also seen guns inside what they had thought were the safe rooms of their lives. The caretaker carried the woodrat outside. "Let me know if you have any more trouble," he said.

Lola will turn it into a story for her morning assignment: "It's hard to trust a man with a chocolate chip cookie in one hand and a loaded gun in the other." At breakfast there will be lots of teasing about the attack of the woodrat in Cabin 6, and I think it's going to go on forever until I find the words to say to the Indian writer from Nespelem who is sitting next to me, a man whose family name is Joseph, "I've lived here, I should have known." Immediately, with a twist of a tourniquet like one of the characters in his reservation EMT stories, he stopped the conversation and guided us back into the morning.

Even as I took my first deep breath I realized the irony. He was a descendant of Chief Joseph's people who had been driven from this high mountain valley by firepower, sheer numbers of soldiers with rifles. As school kids, we were taught not about smallpox and malaria and influenza epidemics but about guns. Gunpowder had purchased our freedom, we were told, enforced our manifest right to this destiny. From the beginning, it seems, guns have defined our relationship to this land we settled ourselves on. And even the Nez Perce, those superb warriors defending themselves against the first attack of the Idaho Volunteers (who shot at them as they rode out to parley under a white flag) with bows and arrows, a few shotguns and muzzle-loaders, mostly muskets—losing no one and killing thirty-three—recognized that without the sixty-three rifles they retrieved from that battlefield, they might not have been able to fight their way through those incredible odds to within a day's journey of safety in Canada.

Numbers. Two hundred seventy million people live in this country, and among us we own an estimated two hundred million guns.

70    Indian people, as nearly as I can see, don't know the answer to the questions raised by guns, either. The Nez Perce and Cayuse, though, and the Walla Walla and Umatilla and Shoshone-Bannock and Paiute, whose warriors fought and continue to fight so hard for survival seem willing to recognize the cost of their guns. At the Tamastslikt Cultural Institute just four miles down the road from my house in Pendleton, for instance, visitors can press a button marked Warriors and see Wish

Patrick describing how his grandfather taught him to hunt. "Never point a rifle at a human being," he had told the boy. In the video Patrick, a gray-haired veteran of the Korean War, still can't tell his story without tears. "I've had a hard time with it," he says. "My grandfather didn't know what was going to happen to me."

# 3

Most of us—rural and urban people, easterners and westerners alike—aren't so willing to face the price we all pay to be a culture supported by guns. A front page local interest story in the *East Oregonian* featured a winter diversion our town is offering: networked "hunt each other down" computer games. "It's especially popular with fathers and sons," said the proprietor, adding that of course it was ridiculous, all this fuss about video games and violence. "It's a *game*," he said. Across the river in Washington the legislature was so bothered by evidence linking gun ownership to increased likelihood of being shot (three times more likely, even after the statisticians have removed other factors like alcoholism or drug abuse, family violence, past arrests) that they closed police files to epidemiologists. And although doctors train at Washington Hospital Center not far from the White House to gain battlefield experience—a situation unique among industrialized nations—Congress has ruled that none of its appropriated funds may be used by the Center for Disease Control to research gun-related injuries, since this research might be interpreted as "advocating or promoting gun control." A few years ago the small southwestern Oregon town of Chiloquin made the papers when its city council passed a law that every adult household was required to own a gun, and this summer our legislature considered making all the towns in our state follow Chiloquin's example. It's the Archie Bunker defense against airline highjackers: arm all the passengers. And silly as that sounds, it may echo one source of our pervasive gun culture. After the Civil War, the U.S. Army sent its obsolete muskets home with the discharged soldiers. Suddenly more of us than ever were armed and dangerous, and the need for defense against each other became very real.

71

In eastern Oregon people are used to guns, and they'd vote against most versions of gun control in a minute. Guns are tools, people here tell each other. Tools we need. But we're as troubled by the news as anybody else, all these guns used and misused by people far away from injured colts and coyotes. Forty thousand people are killed with guns every year in the country we have claimed with the technology of gunpowder. The summer after my father died *Time* ran a story simply printing the photos of all the people who had been killed that week —either by themselves or by others—and there were 454 photos or white spaces where not even a photo was left. This was a decade before the school shootings that made the papers, though there were already plenty of school shootings, children holding their mothers' hands on the way to school hit by stray bullets, kids whose schools had given up on them shooting each other on other playgrounds. Then one of the most shocking school shootings happened in our state, in a town not unlike our own. A boy's first .22 rifle. A locker check at the high school a few miles north of us produced thirty-eight guns, and there had been an armed confrontation in the school's parking lot between the kids in cowboy hats and long black dusters and the Mexican kids. Last spring Indian students were encouraged to skip the last day of our middle school after a gun threat aimed specifically at them. This isn't even counting the twelve-year-old just west of us who died when the gun fired as he and his friends were climbing out of the car after the trip to town, white kids searching out Mexican kids, baby gangs, or the other eleven-year-old who killed his best friend with a pellet gun fired at close range (*a gun is always loaded*). Or the fourteen-year-old in Kennewick who shot and killed his teacher, or the drive-by shootings in Pasco. Just last month, a few days before Christmas, two people were found shot to death in a car in nearby Hermiston—two more were arrested—and this week we read of a murder-suicide there. The people involved in these stories were seventeen, eighteen, nineteen. The oldest was twenty-three. They leave babies, toddlers, mothers and lovers and friends. I know them, or know someone who does. Yesterday grief counselors were called in to the elementary school just down the street to help the first-through-fifth graders deal with the

72

loss of their friend Billy, three days short of his ninth birthday, shot with a .22 by his father.

We're not oblivious. We enroll our children in hunter safety classes and read the headlines about the nerve gas leaks just west of us, the sirens that don't work, the false alarm sign flashing on the freeway reader board. Even the big guns, we know all too well, don't always work right.

We know, too, that homes with guns are five times more likely to be the place where a suicide happens than homes without guns. In my town, it's hard to find a home without guns, and it's hard to find someone who doesn't know a family where "five times more likely" conjures up a human face. The high incidence of suicide is a chilling fact in the rural West. Suicide makes its way out of the muffled obituaries in our local newspaper only if it's a child, or if someone has chosen the railroad tracks instead.

And sometimes, we have to admit, those shootings that seem as far away from us as *NYPD Blue* happen right under our windows. We've had our first freeway shooting, and last summer on an afternoon when the downtown pavement held the shimmering heat between the buildings and we were all waiting for sunset and relief, a tired officer on the end of his shift stopped a man named Walks-On-Top just a block short of his apartment—the car seemed to be weaving, he said later—and suddenly the cop had a bullet in his leg and Walks-On-Top was dead.

After the gas station shootout we had plenty to say. The *East Oregonian* carried the story for days, probing it from every angle, touching the edges of the wound like unbelieving fingers counting stitches, hundreds and hundreds of stitches across what had once been such smooth human skin.

Josh had just left his swing shift behind the counter of the BP station. He ran the truck's engine in the parking lot for a while, waiting for the heater's warmth for the drive home. He missed it by twelve minutes.

I'd been worried, of course, about robbery. The BP service station/mini mart is just off the freeway exit, it's open all night, and there is beer in the coolers. But I hadn't imagined this: a man and his girlfriend using the station as a fortress for a shootout with the police. They had

73

kidnapped their children from foster care in his own mother's house, shooting their way through his stepfather's resistance and leaning out of the car to fire back at pursuing police, pulling into the BP on rims after the freeway chase had spiked their tires. So the clerk who had just replaced Josh was the one who huddled with the girlfriend and the four children on the floor between the breath mints and the Fritos while the police blazed at the man shooting from the open doorway and the children screamed.

I left school the next afternoon, as soon as I'd heard the news from one of my students. *He's okay, they'd have called me by now*. Big glass panels in the door and one of the windows had been replaced by sheets of plywood, and I walked past bullet holes pitting the walls beneath the glass, bullet holes across the entire front of the station. Yellow paint outlined a non-human shape in the doorway. Smaller yellow circles spread out across the asphalt. People carrying Big Gulp cups, their tickets to the show, milled around the doorway, poking at the painted circles with their boots. Finally I saw Josh coming out from behind the counter, his face pale, those eyes, coming to meet me, both of us holding each other, just holding on, not speaking.

"Ghouls," he said, finally, looking over my shoulder at the people outside. His voice sounded like the singers on those scratched wind-up phonograph 78's I found in the old log cabin when I was a kid, high and far away, even though it was right in my ear.

Here's what didn't make the paper, he showed me. There are always two attendants on duty, and the younger boy had come out from the storeroom. He was standing in his place behind the counter during all this gunfire. The automatic teller machine had deflected the police bullets that would have killed him.

But none of the (how many? fifty? a hundred and fifty? the man was using an assault rifle; the three police shooters all had shotguns) hurtling pieces of lead went into the children, the girlfriend, the BP workers. Or the police. None of them even went into the attendants or customers at the Texaco station across the street, or into people who happened to be driving by. None of them went into my son. Several did, of course, go into the man in the doorway, and our newspaper quoted the official analysis, several paragraphs long, of exactly where they lodged and which of them had actually killed him. Maybe the editor knew we all needed to put down the paper and walk away with a physical fact, something we thought we could understand.

"He was howling at the police," the older BP worker told the newspaper reporter. "He was yelling about his son, how they couldn't take his little boy away from him." "Eric thought they'd taken his kids away because he was poor," the man's brother said later. "Christmas had really gotten to him. He'd promised the kids they'd all be together for Christmas."

I don't shoot any more. But once in a while Dean smiles and says something about "you and Annie Oakley," and I feel my heart leap up. For a moment I am that twelve-year-old again, the girl who needed to be real. And I can still remember how it felt when the whirling clay birds fell out of the sky, the closest I would ever come to magic.

Real, and magic? How is it, I wonder, that shooting can give us that feeling—that illusion of such oneness with the world—when the rifle racks in our pickup trucks are such an obvious barrier, a blue steel fence we keep between us and that world? You can't control the world and *be* the world at the same time.

But control is the seed of our stories, a seed so deeply planted it volunteers new shoots in every weather. Technology can save us. We will program each gun so that only its owner can shoot it. Pretty simple, really. And we can pass tougher laws, prosecute the people who don't keep their guns locked safely away. We can get a handle on this gun violence problem. But I keep thinking of the school shootings: Kip Kinkel did own his .22, and the little boys in Arkansas had to break into the family's locked gun cabinet to kill their classmates. Besides, if guns are tools, they are specialized tools. Hunters use a different gauge shotgun for each kind of bird, and for skeet vs. trap shooting; .30-.30's shoot deer through thick brush at closer range while .270's and .300's shoot across the canyon at elk—so it's easy to picture the household arsenals that would develop in the West if we couldn't share, if each of us had to have our own.

75

In my family, at least, the problem lies deeper. In a sense, the NRA is right: it's not the guns, it's the people. But it's a lot more people than they are willing to acknowledge. *A gun is always loaded*, said my father, and he might as well have said *the story I am passing on, this legend I am handing you, is cocked and primed, set to explode.*

# Tracking My Father

"That place destroyed me," Dad said. "And it will destroy you too." He had lifted his head from the stem of pain it rested on to look directly at me, his hand gripping the wooden armrest of the Morris chair. It was like standing under a snow-laden pine just as it thawed enough to drop its heavy load onto my head and shoulders. That same shivering shock.

I knew, of course, that he wanted to sell the place. The homestead he had fought so stubbornly to hold on to now pulled like a stone weight on his curving spine. But Mom was refusing to let it go. Nearly ten years before, when the Dworshak Dam was completed, they had left the ranch to follow her job with Corps of Engineers around the inland Northwest, renting out the house and fields to a series of families nearly as poor as ours had been. He was fifty-nine that year, already on Social Security because he had worked so hard that the cushioning between his vertebrae had worn away. He grew flowers in a series of trailer courts, teased the neighborhood children, went to yard sales. He even bought a bicycle. If it weren't for the Old Grandad in the cup of coffee in his hand all day and the long, dark silences of his afternoons and evenings—even in those first few years before the asthma and emphysema had tightened their grip on his chest—I would have said he was happy. Now that Mom's retirement was nearing she wanted to go home, as they had always planned. For her the home place meant the smell of syringa and chinook wind and whitetail deer coming down to the pond; for him it had come to mean something else.

I hadn't said much in this debate, but it was obvious that I couldn't imagine it. The home place, gone? The east field turned into five-acre home-and-horse-stable housing, the upper forty into view sites? It seemed as impossible as the Clearwater disappearing. How would we know when it was spring without the sound of February blackbirds down by the pond or lamb's tongues turning the hill yellow just above the mailbox? My brothers and sister must have felt the same kind of puzzled fogginess, trying to grasp such an idea. But it was only me he was talking to.

I looked at my father, wanting, as always, to wrap his anguish in solace; to nod, feeling his guidance settling like a compass in my chest, pointing me safely through the cold journey toward true north. At the same moment, though—and this was a pull as strong as gravity—I wanted to turn and walk away. It was almost physical, an urge to run down this hill, my arms out to catch the sky; to sing into the lifting wind, fly steady as a raven straight away from these words. From whatever it was that always made his eyes say No.

*Dad, I can't follow you down that road*, I wanted to say. But what if I could, what if I was already halfway down it? The truth is, I'd been following him since I was old enough to walk. Every Saturday when he rose from the breakfast table and hunched into his jacket, I was pulling my boots on too, trailing him out to the barn, down to the woods, across the east field—wherever he was going that day. I remember walking behind him in the dark, stretching my stride to step into holes in the snow left by his buckle overshoes just at the edge of the lantern light. I missed every third boot print, then caught my balance and reached again for the rhythm of his stride. I carried an extra stick of stovewood on top of the pile already crushing my plaid wool sleeves, stacked the pickup load of mill-ends he had tossed into a heap, pulled barbed wire tight while he attached the fence stretchers, dropped two corn kernels into the center of every hole while he balanced the earth on his waiting hoe. The first time I helped with the haying, forking aside piles of new-cut alfalfa where it grew too thick before he pulled the mower back up over the rise of the east field for the next swath, he smiled and said he couldn't have done it without me. But that was the summer before the quarrel over the ranch. After that, all he ever said was, "You've got young legs—slip up to the garage and get me the long-handled pliers."

78

Now, with gray was streaking my hair as well as his, I still didn't know how to talk to my father. I wasn't even sure what he meant. Maybe he was talking about work, how he'd worked his life away on the ranch. Or that terrible fight with his mother. Was he reminding me that his children's generation was no more immune to such family struggles—and the need for love and acceptance, the self-worth we come to think winning these battles will guarantee—than he had been? Maybe he meant that the home place could potentially destroy each of us, luring us with its promise to heal whatever our individual pains might be.

What kept me silent were those same old feelings: respect, love, anguish for his pain. That chilling fear that he might be right.

Some of the stories I remember, some I see as images that I may have imagined to go with the words. Dad pounding cedar fence posts into the earth with a sledgehammer the day he got all his teeth pulled for a complete set of dentures. It's what needed doing that day, he said. Or scooping snow in an arc over his head, shoveling another trench from the little board house to the barn the winter I was three, when the snow fell so deep that it was taller than he was. The world had closed over his head, but he walked through it anyway. He had to. "Work" wasn't just a place where he went, I already knew. It was who he was. Mama worked hard too, of course. She scrubbed Dad's jeans on a washboard and ironed ruffles into the scratchy dresses I hated with a flatiron heated on the cookstove, but she laughed, too, and sang, and took us outside to look at the stars. There would be a cookie saved for each of us in Dad's black lunch bucket when Jill and I ran to meet him at the gate and share the bumpy ride back down the hill to the house. He smelled like the dry cheese sandwich-half in its melted wax paper, and his shirt was damp with sweat. That spring he had taken a job at the planer mill. It was steadier than woods work—he was thirty-three; already he'd worked in the woods for twenty years—and now that he had a family he needed a regular paycheck. Is there harder work than setting chokers, bumping knots on the landing, leaning over one end of a crosscut saw? But loading green dimension lumber into boxcars was not easy, either. When I was four we moved to town for the winter, the four of us and then the baby crowded into a one-room house so Jill could go to school, but Dad still had to battle the winter road up the mountain twice a day to do the chores, feeding and milking, breaking ice on the pond. One morning he came back home only a

79

few minutes after he had left us and sat down without speaking. Finally he told Mom, "I got to the junction and I couldn't remember where I was headed, the ranch or the mill. I can't seem to get my bearings."

It scared me, and I could see it scared Mama too. Dad was the one who kept going no matter how tired he got. "Why doesn't he ever get sick?" I remember asking when I was eight or nine. I had never seen him spend a day in bed. It was still dark all those mornings when his pickup pulled up onto the main road and we watched the headlights tracing a thin beam against the firs until they disappeared where the road turned by the old rock crusher. After his long day at the mill—by the time I was in junior high he was past the days of pulling on the green chain and graveyard shifts inside boxcars, but lumber grading meant standing for eight hours, boards flying out at him, alert for the sudden scream of a broken belt and the jagged shrapnel of slivered wood; turning each plank, the red and blue lumber chalk wearing down like his vertebrae, the tendons in his wrists and fingers paralyzed with pain—after all that, there was more waiting for him at home. Five of us kids, each of us with glasses fragile as the thin skim of ice on the watering trough. Was he ever not paying for somebody's broken lens? And always that disease that haunted our family, the asthma that could put his sons in the hospital, bring them right to the edge of death and push down on their breastbones if you let them outside for a minute to run or feel the wind in their faces. Or even if you kept them inside. I remember hearing Mom and Dad struggling to pay each bill at the kitchen table when the mill dropped its medical insurance and three thousand dollars out of his yearly income of forty-five hundred went to doctor bills to keep all three boys breathing. There were the goats to milk—every night, every morning—because the boys were allergic to cow's milk, and the cow to milk and steers to feed, and the chickens, the feeder pigs, the garden. All this meant fences pulled to the earth as if gravity had a grudge against him, and machines to crank and cuss and baby along, carburetors smelling up the kitchen table in the dim lamplight. July brought those double shifts in the hayfield and then at the mill, and his "vacation pay"—the extra check he got for working straight through August—bought school clothes for the year.

80

"Worked himself to death." It's still all too common an expression where I live. My father had grown up in a community that measured land with chains and gauged a man's worth by the number of foot-pounds he could move from here to there—the competence of his hands. But "competence" and "competition" share the same root in our language, like either/or answers to a trick question on the big exam. Senator Dawes's argument that selfishness fueled the fires of progress—and the resulting Allotment Act that had led our family to this land—gave with one hand and struck with the other. Men like my father were competent, but if civilization meant banks and progress meant bank accounts, they could not compete. The harder Dad worked at his manual labor, the more he condemned himself. He could see it happening, of course—but he didn't know how to stop it.

The summer I was fifteen I kept a journal, a conscious effort at sanity now that school was out. It's a painful read—determinedly optimistic, taking my father's side when he broke his silence with bitter jokes even as I remained loyal to my mother's version of reality. Especially haunting are the lists of chores I inventoried each day: "Today I cleaned the barn, rototilled the garden, ironed for two hours, packed buckets of water to the new fruit trees. When Dad came home all he said was, 'This yard's a mess. Doesn't anybody ever lift a finger around here?'" The journal ends in July, leaving a book full of blank pages.

Then, midway through the summer I was sixteen, he quit working. Of course, he still got up every morning at five and drove down the hill to do the job he had hated for years, but when he got home he sat down in the green-webbed chaise lawn chair we had given him for father's day and opened the first extra-tall can of beer. We had never seen him drink. "Sorry, I can't," had always been his polite and embarrassed refusal. "I got to be a regular alcoholic when I was a kid working in the woods." The stories from those drinking days had seemed as distant as the childhood tales of jumping off the barn holding the big umbrella or sledding right through the barbed wire fence that had ripped open both his leather mittens. Who was this man who stretched out his legs in the black-walnut shade until the crickets sang us into darkness? Sitting there with a beer can propped on the waist of his jeans—lying there, really—he didn't even look the same. In the

81

stories he had told—just pages torn from larger stories—alcohol had made him a different person. Was he dangerous? The tiller sat stalled in the center of the garden, a reproach he ignored while I tried to keep the two acres cultivated with just a hoe. I was already doing the milking and feeding but what if the cows got foot-rot or bloat, or hardwared the way Polly had last May? Sometimes I walked across the garden to the log cabin under the firs and stared at the notched logs fitted together so tightly. He had built it, with no help from his own father, when he was no older than I was. My hands felt empty in the pockets of my jeans.

Late that fall, Dad got up from the supper table and walked out into the garden. The garden tiller was beyond repair now, he said. He couldn't believe I'd just left it there in the open like that. Tom helped me drag it back through the corn stubble and under the barbed wire fence to the shed, both of us jerking when the tines caught a blackened squash vine or a ridge of dirt, our elbows and knees bumping into each other. "Shit!" "Christ!" We kept our voices low, almost as if we were swearing at each other.

Once you start saying words like these, I had discovered that summer, it's hard to stop. Fury swam in my mouth with spiny fins, leaped out into the empty air at unexpected moments. Yet I couldn't forget all those haying seasons, waiting in the haydust with my pitchfork and blistered hands and watching my father's face burned darker each time he turned to look over his shoulder and the old Cletrac jolted forward until this load, too, rose and caught and swung into the barn. The harder he worked, I had thought, watching, the more others who didn't have to work so hard—I pictured them all as men, in cool white short-sleeved shirts—were willing to see him as a mass of bone and muscle to heave the world's weight for their profit. I was still arguing a silent case for him, defending my father in the courtrooms of my mind, a youthful Marxist at the barricades of the Cold War. He always took a few minutes to unlace his work boots and step into his Romeo slippers before supper, but the boots stood against the wall behind his chair as he ate.

It had been obvious for a long time, the sharp-toothed trap that lay in wait beneath the promises of the work ethic. Yet the message I still told myself was simple. Work harder. *Make* it work. People were dying in the South, shot in the back of the head. Even as I was forking hay to the cows or pouring the warm bucket of milk through the strainer, there were bodies, burned and bleeding, hanging from the trees. Answers were blowing in the wind, Bob Dylan told me. People with dreams were working to their deaths to achieve them. For their children, or their parents, or for someone they didn't even know. What were daily ten-hour shifts in Syringa Café, then, pumping gas and washing dishes and cleaning toilets between customers, compared to that? If it was the only way I could get to college and learn what I had to know. I knew it was a paradox, but I didn't know any way out of it. Hard work could change what was wrong with the world. Couldn't it? It had to.

College meant five hours of sleep, maybe, and two hundred scoops of hard-frozen ice cream and an aching wrist, eating dinner with the dorm's kitchen crew squeezed between the steam table and the smell of the scouring stone as it scraped that night's grease into the catch tray beneath the big grill, but the diploma and the Phi Beta Kappa key at the end of those years were only illusions; I would have to work harder still. Teaching was the most difficult thing I'd ever done. Lesson plans and grading were the least of it. Every bell meant a new space of time to shape into meaning, Indian and Mexican and white kids asking questions with their eyes.

I had left that first teaching job to go back to graduate school when I met the man I knew I would marry. We would make a different kind of family: unlike my father, Dean could laugh and cry. He was creative and perceptive and compassionate. He talked in metaphors. Of course, it would be hard work, this life out there ahead of us. He drank too much—but that would change now that he was with me. It was 1972, an easy time to believe that what I would later learn to call post-traumatic stress was a natural reaction of a good man to whatever had happened while he was in the army. And his mother had died in his arms when he was fifteen, leaving only an empty pill bottle. But now someone loved him.

When we drove home that summer, a three-day trek with my shepherd dog and everything I owned in a blue Ford Falcon as we set

83

off to start our lives together, Dad wouldn't speak to him. In the pre-dawn hours of the morning, unable to face another silent meal at the kitchen table, we got up and drove away. "Why did you bring me here?" Dean asked as we pulled up onto the county road. I couldn't quite put my answer into words. But I knew it had something to do with the earth. I had wanted to pull it close around us, bury our faces in it. "Like a snake-bit dog," the saying I'd heard while I was growing up. I wanted this land to heal us both. The windows were rolled down and I breathed in as deeply as I could.

After the summer my father spent stretching his aching legs in the late afternoon shade and drinking beer while light faded from the skyline—his one-man strike, as I had begun to think of it—he finally stood up again and walked back into our lives. He worked steadily now, but not as if the chore would ever be finished or as if anything would really change even if it were. When the mill closed, he took a job as a school custodian—my top-team crosscut sawyer father, a janitor—and finally finished out his working years in the heat of the oiling truck on the county road crew, his face white from the pain of that damaged spine. Between these jobs were a couple of six-month stretches of unemployment, jobs for a man turned fifty scarce now that the big trees had been taken. He filled the hours by learning to antique a wooden table and chair set—finally Mom would have something more than a plywood sheet attached to the old chrome table legs as our family had grown—and drinking. The doctored cup of coffee looked exactly like the one he had always braced himself against, leaning on his forearms at the end of the kitchen table. The difference was the way it let things slip by him, just minnows brushing against his calves in a cool stream. But as the hours went on the current began to take him down with it, like the sucking eddies in the river that haunted his dreams, to that dark soundless place where he was alone. "It will pull you under," he had told us again and again, story after story about that river.

The undertow. I had felt it too—not in water but on land, our land. Like the night Dad took the lantern and left us in the barn, Jill and

84

Tom and me. Outside we could hear muffled grunts, a whirl of snarl and growl—Tippy was fighting with a bear. "I need to get to the house and get the rifle," Dad told us. "I'll have to take the lantern with me— but you'll be okay here in the barn. Keep the door shut. You're safe here. That dog of yours is so brave he'll never back off. He needs some help—a bear will kill a dog." It was the most explaining he had ever done, and the most gentle. He was grinning a little, I remember, as he hooked the chain over the nail to latch the big barn door and then the crack of light vanished. Outside, that noise. Tom was little; I was eight, nearly nine. We bumped into each other, lost in blackness. "All these barn windows are open," Jill said. "A bear could climb up the manure pile and come right through!"

"But Dad said—"

"Shhh!" Tom was whimpering. We all held our breaths. Silence. Maybe the bear was already in the barn, behind us in the stanchions. Maybe it was coming toward us on the plank floor.

"What was that?"

When we broke for the light in the kitchen window I can't remember if we latched the barn door behind us. I do remember Dad running toward us, the rifle in one hand and the swinging lantern in the other, and then Tippy coming up out of the darkness. The bear was gone. But the dog—my dog, really—was bruised and limping, and I knew he was lucky to be alive. "He was the best dog we ever had until he tangled with that bear," Dad would say later. "You kids wouldn't stay in the barn and I couldn't get out there quick enough to help him, but he had a lot of heart when he was a pup, Tip did."

"I'm not afraid of a thing," Dad said. "Except rattlesnakes." Mom shook her head, but it would take me longer to see it. His fear of letting us drive, or even ride in cars with anyone else. His panic on one-way streets or in any kind of traffic. Making my way through an unfamiliar airport to change planes one morning, I suddenly realized how long it has taken me to let go of these lessons and simply follow the signs through the corridors. I still have trouble lighting Coleman lanterns or pilot lights. "Weren't you afraid of getting kicked?" a friend asked me recently when I told her about my 4-H steers, and there it was again, the memory of those nights in my bed staring at the reflected firelight shifting across the ceiling and telling myself that in spite of all those warnings about the dangers of working close to cattle I could do this. I could. Some people find pigs so fascinating that they make them pets, but my first instinct will always be to pull in my toes. "Get back!—that sow'll eat your feet right off!" For my father, the earth was a dangerous place. You kids stay inside this fence. You can ride the horse, from the house to the gate over there, and back—straight across the pasture—but no saddle, you might get hung up and dragged. You can't take the bike out on the county road until you've shown me you can ride it across the plowed field. Keep off the woodshed roof, stay out of those trees; don't swim in the river. *Watch for snakes!*

Late one night, years past the boundaries of my childhood, Dad and I sat at my kitchen table. Dean and Josh had gone to bed; it was one of the two or three times that he would let me glimpse the man behind the grin that appeared whenever he was afraid. "I couldn't have friends," he told me. "It was just too dangerous." He was shaking his head, remembering. "I knew they would come along like they did that time, they just picked me up, one under each arm. If I wanted to quit drinking I couldn't let myself have friends." He cradled his midnight coffee mug with both hands.

At the spring root feast in the longhouse near Pendleton, like the root feasts that will be happening along the Clearwater, men will serve the deer and elk and salmon, women the roots and chokecherries and huckleberries. Then all the people can eat. "Next time, invite a man," the elder Cecelia Bearchum told me after she had visited my classroom one May morning. "You need men's stories, too." Seventy percent of North American native peoples were matrilineal and matriarchal. But matriarchy didn't mean absolute power for women, the way patriarchy in my own culture seemed to place all real power in the hands of men. I'm not sure what it meant. An acknowledgment of change, perhaps, of constant flow, even as a people leaned deeply into the permanence of the land. Patriarchy—the 1950's kind—was different. Change was not something people learned from the land but something they did to the land. Strong men wrested farms from swamp or glacial rock fields, channeled and harnessed the rivers, managed the forests into clear cuts, and replanted stands of new growth as uniform as eighth-grade girls in their spring dresses at the first afternoon dance in the gym.

At school the teachers drew vertical lines on the blackboards: the Great Chain of Being, we wrote in our notebooks. The man at the top of the school's chain was called the principal. We sat in straight lines, eyes to the front. Even today I am surprised to see newspaper photos of elementary school principals on the playground with the kids, pushing a boy in a swing or teaching a girl to hold a bat. The rules in my own childhood were rigid, and challenges—or perceived challenges; most of them were just mistakes—to the power of any hierarchy, even the one who sat at the head of his own supper table, were met with physical power, rituals designed to remind the offender at each blow of the pain of getting out of line. If you get in trouble at school, you're in trouble at home, too, Dad told us. I remember the long walk to the principal's office in sixth grade—three of us had refused to complete what we thought was an unfair punitive spelling assignment—and the adrenaline that lifted me into throat-tightening terror when Barbara's giggles turned hysterical as we stood in front of his big blonde desk. But we weren't beaten. "Because we're *girls?*" we whispered to each other on the way back to the classroom: a long, floating walk, our feet still unsteady on the gray tiled hallway. We were already bitter about the double standard, of course, but the boys had to live with another kind of doubleness. When they broke their knuckles against the walls of their childhoods none of us knew whether they'd be getting a Scout badge or twenty-five "hacks" with Mr. Simmons's paddle—which playground rumors said was made of both wood and leather. Male or female, there was no escaping the price of patriarchy.

Living under my father's roof, the atmosphere in the house molding itself around his voice—or his silence (*No loud, sudden sounds: don't drop that stack of cream separator trays!*)—I knew there was more to his story. He wasn't just a father to be feared and obeyed. He too had been a child. I had watched his face when he told us about his mother's razor strap, and we could all picture him as the little boy growing into his

87

own father's shadow—never quite able to please his dad, we could tell in those smoky stories he told us over the Sunday morning breakfast table, syrup and bacon rinds hardening on our plates. He had climbed on the stanchions to harness the team when he was only six, plowing, seeding the fields while his father was away in the woods. Once, he said, he had used all the seed on half the field, the arc of his arm not as strong as a man's though he was doing a man's work.

He would have been fourteen and "batching" downtown to go to high school on October 29, 1929, when the world caved in around him. I could see him as a young man struggling to find a place: at the end of a crosscut saw, at the end of a bottle on rowdy weekends away from the lumber camps, at the bottom of a ravine in that car full of dead and dying CCC boys. After months in a body cast in the Boise hospital, they released him into a December snowstorm. He had no money and could barely walk. He hitchhiked as far as Grangeville, where the sheriff let him sleep in the jail overnight to keep from freezing. He was eighteen.

It was easy to envision Dad as the twenty-year-old who saw my mother's picture in his sister Edith's scrapbook and said, "That's the girl I'm going to marry." There was no money for dates, but she seemed to love singing in the dark as they walked around town, hand in hand. Sometimes they rode in the truck with Edie and her boyfriend, all four of them singing. When we were junior high age Jill and I would invite the neighbors over without telling the folks—who might say oh no, not tonight—because Edna always brought her fiddle and maybe Mom and Dad would smile at each other and we'd hear their voices blending together. *We ain't got a barrel of money, maybe we're ragged and funny, but we'll travel along, singing a song, side by side...* ("Do you love me?" he would ask my mother when they were young. "Poor boy," she says, now. "Nobody had ever really loved him.")

I had trailed my dad around the ranch for enough miles to know what he wanted. He was working hard for the reward that would never come. The hand reaching down that rigid Chain of Being to touch his shoulder. *Good man. Well done.*

After his mother died, Dad's sisters found an handful of arrowheads wrapped in a handkerchief at the back of a drawer. He had given them to his mother on Mother's Day the year he was six—every piece of beauty he had pulled from the earth behind the plow, his total wealth. "Bud, check these out," Aunt Grace wrote on the envelope, pushing hard to get him to accept something, anything, from his mother's belongings. No, he said. He wanted nothing.

*That place will destroy you.* I want to argue, rebel against my father's wisdom the way I finally began to do at seventeen. *No, Dad. No. This can't be what the land is saying. Listen to the wind. The lookout quail, the mourning dove, the redtail. We have learned to hear the whispers of snow; maybe we can learn to hear the song waiting for each of us.... your song, Dad, did your song ever come to you?*

The night after my father died, the house where I had grown up filling with uncles and young cousins and darkness, Josh decided he wanted to spend the night down in the woods. He had made a pole structure just below the east field ("I've got a surprise for you, Mom," he had told me, his eyes shining gray the way they did sometimes just at evening). It looked like a small longhouse, with lodgepoles lashed together in half circles at each end.

Josh had been driving his Uncle John's '41 Chevy pickup around the fields that summer, learning to shift. In the dusk of that evening Dean and I stood together, watching the rust-colored truck circle across the drying pasture and dip below the curve of the field. "I need to be down there tonight, Mom," he had said. Finally I went inside. He'd be stretching out his sleeping bag in the dry grass under the poles now. I remembered all those afternoons beneath the old-growth Ponderosas in the hum of pine beetles and the wind-river sound coming up out of the Whiskey Creek canyon, listening for those voices I still wanted to hear. *This is where I'll build my own house someday,* I had thought. I was fourteen that summer, too. The stars had been out for nearly an hour when we saw the narrow headlights cutting a track back across the field and went out to meet him. "I couldn't do it," Josh said. "I just felt so alone."

89

For people in the Pacific Northwest, the winter of 1996 is one of those times by which we will measure our lives. Rivers out of their banks ripped through woodpiles and plywood barriers, street signs emerged from the water on a Main Street shopping district, whole mountains thundered down on sleeping families in their houses. A warm, wet storm—what we learned that year to call a Pineapple Express—had blown in on a country already saturated with rain and deep, wet snow, the soil not yet frozen. And the world fell apart in ways we had not imagined. Sections of roads as long as chip trucks crumpled and slid into waiting canyons. The earth opened into sinkholes that swallowed homes and cars. Big Canyon Creek came roaring down toward the Clearwater, rolling D-9 Caterpillars and houses and boulders toward the bridge across the highway, which vanished instantly, gone in a gulping swallow of mud and crashing froth. Someone counted forty-two slides blocking Highway 12 between Lewiston and Kamiah, the next town upriver from Orofino. Six closed the road up the hill toward home. Mom and Jill huddled at the ranch, which still had electricity and a propane-burning stove, and waited.

Before the authorities could forbid such a thing, someone laid a steel truck bed across the gaping hole over Big Canyon Creek, and people along the Clearwater had one-lane access to their medical appointments in Lewiston while the real repairs were made and the community learned the language of FEMA and tried to help their neighbors. But for a long time, all over the Northwest, the land kept sliding.

The first time I made my way up the river to the ranch, dodging that morning's rocks and keeping an eye on the pines leaning out at new angles from the bank above me, I saw the home place as if some filtering layer had been washed away. Benchland, with a steep ridge rising above it. Our bench falls off into another ridge, and then another bench, before the vertical walled canyons of Whiskey Creek and Orofino Creek and the river itself. I knew the benchlands had been formed by slides, but I had no idea how sudden and powerful these slides must have been. How massive. This land had been sliding for a long time.

Yet this new vision was familiar, too. I recognized it like a lost memory. In the first years after my father's death the earth under my own feet had seemed to be slipping sideways. There were so many places that could collapse and pull me under. Suicide isn't catching, I wanted to tell people who looked at me more carefully than before, and yet I too watched the ones I loved as if only my gaze would keep them upright and breathing. Anyone could vanish, overnight. They were flowers, plants swaying on such slender stems. Especially Josh, who had just graduated from the eighth grade and was walking toward the double doors of high school that summer.

"You used to think I made some pretty big mistakes," Dad had said from his hospital bed on his last Father's Day, looking up from the card I had given him. The wide yellow brace circled his rib cage. A memory, bright with adolescent rage: I am gripping the edge of the kitchen table, standing above the steaming supper plates. *You're ruining my brothers' lives!* "I'm a parent now," I told him, and he leaned forward just a little on the hospital bed, as if a weight had shifted. He smiled. It was as close as we would come to apologies.

I didn't know the half of it yet. Tonight my neighbors are putting up their Christmas lights, and watching the little cottage across the street from me outlining its roof and windows in blinking color, I think about those Christmases when I felt nothing but grief in this season of birth, this celebration of Mother and Son. Out on the main highways are tinseled "SEASON'S GREETINGS" signs; silhouettes of gold bells and faded red Santas lean out from each intersection. There were years when I thought I could not endure this glitter hanging over my head from early November until mid-January while the darkness grew like a fungus. Even the snow seemed to settle already yellowed with mud and gravel. The only Christmas decoration that didn't make my heart clench was the red breast of the finch at the feeder.

A small white star hangs in the plum tree just next door, a soft glow that takes me back to my own childhood in the little house lit only by kerosene lamps. Our brothers haven't been born yet; my sister and I are small. Outside is the milky way and a kerosene lantern to guide us through the darkness to the barn, but sometimes we beg Dad for our favorite kind of magic. "Take me to town to see the lights?" Winding down the mountain grade, we can see what looks like a skyful of colored stars below us. Then we are in the town itself, neon oranges and greens and pinks flashing all around.

91

At Christmas time that light blossomed everywhere. From the trees and lawns, from the rooftops. The big log house at the top of the town kids' sledding hill lit up the sky, and Dad always detoured from the street that led to Grammie's house so we could see it up close.

Near the end of his life, when his asthma and emphysema and depression were pressing on his chest, my father didn't want the fuss of Christmas either. It was different, though, when we were growing up. It happened every December, yet I couldn't have been more amazed if he had pulled a flock of chortling doves out of the black felt crusher he wore cocked over his left eye. He brought home bags of store-bin chocolates, boxes filled with tangerines and hard candy to hide on the porch until Christmas Eve. He led the expedition across the field for the Christmas tree he had picked out in July. He ate platefuls of peanut brittle and fudge and divinity and taffy all by himself. He laughed, he sang carols. He poked a stiff finger through the bowl of nuts. Somehow, we knew, he and Mom would manage to stretch the heavy blanket of poverty that hung over us enough to find a present for each of us, something perfect. Sleds and dolls and model airplanes and basketballs and wood burners and paint sets, one year a coping saw, a gift that honored me as I struggled through my splitting-applebox wooden projects. Always an orange in the toe of our stockings, and a pack of Blackjack gum, Juicy Fruit and Lifesavers; Mom's warm cinnamon rolls for breakfast. The candle-shaped light on the top of our tree bubbled when it got hot enough, and I remember sitting in the dark of the room lit only by Christmas lights and burning candles as we waited for the bubbles to start climbing up the blue glass stem, trying to hold so still that this night would never end and we'd always have this father, the one who stomped snow off his boots and grinned.

Soon my youngest brother Monte's Christmas box will arrive in the mail. Some years he sends the cookies in a Tupperware container; sometimes they arrive hard and broken, wrapped in wax paper in a battered cardboard box. We sift through the layers, looking for our favorites: the chocolate pinwheels, a gingerbread man with a leg still soft enough to chew. I wonder if his kids still help with the frosting and sprinkles and red-hots.

Monte has spent much of his life as a stay-at-home dad; both Kitty and he have worked hard to be good parents. "I've figured out how to get along with Aaron," Monte joked recently. "Find out what he wants to do, and then offer to help him do it." I don't really know why I keep watching for signs of tension between this father and his children. If it happens, I find myself thinking tonight—if Monte has to wrestle an angel so heavy that no tinseled tree will bear its weight . . . and suddenly I realize that it's Monte I'm worried about, not my niece or nephews. And although it's dark here at my window and I'm looking at the lights across the street and the lights beyond them, cars and trucks coming down Reith Ridge over on the horizon, what I'm seeing is that man last summer, the man who for a moment I thought was Dad still walking down the bright August sidewalk. Tears push at the back of my eyes again, and I remember how my hands had left the steering wheel of my car, how they were reaching for the door handle before they knew what my head was already telling them: you can't leap from your car at a stoplight and gather him up in your arms, *my father, my father.*

Then I feel Dean's hands on my shoulders. I lean back and pull his arms around me, still facing the darkness outside. "Your dad just needed the right medication," he says, finally. I turn into his embrace. Paul Winter's *Winter Solstice* is playing; I think of needle-thin icicles on the Christmas firs. Depression is an imbalance that can be righted before the whole tree crashes into its shadow and we feel the earth quiver under our feet. Maybe it's as simple as that.

When the sun rolls down the ridge to the home place above the Clearwater, it still touches the log cabin first. Light blazes back to me from the lone window. I am usually up early, a camera in my hand—in the spring or with October grasses rising bronze against the sill logs, or snow loading the firs and pine that curve above the roof like an Anasazi cliff. Sometimes, framing the cabin from yet another angle, I can almost see my father. There are traces of his hands on the notched logs and draw-knife shingles and in the mud daubed between the logs. His words of prophesy follow me around the field like ghost breath. As a parent, a teacher, a woman walking this earth, what tracks will my own footprints leave? It's my own journey that I'm on now.

93

Homeless

# Following the Deer

The deer were thick the summer that we waited for my father to die. We were still in the middle of the worst drought in years: an open winter the year before; no snow, no winterkill. Dean and Josh and I had watched the new fawns from the living-room window that June, when we'd first moved back to the old house where I had grown up. And every evening we'd see them coming down the slope, whitetail does and last year's fawns—towheads, Dad had always called them. We tied fluorescent orange and pink streamers to the garden fence, but by August they had stripped the potato vines, smashed the buttercup squash open with their hooves. The corn, of course, they ate while it was still green and tender. And the onions. That was the field garden, the one we tilled in the part of the pasture where it would grow without water. Or rather, where it would water itself, the strip of earth between the baked timothy grass and the old firs that was moist in your hand when everything else was dust. You can't grow a garden that far from the house, Mom reminded us. You don't have a dog. The deer will get it. She had a small garden plot in the trailer court down by the river where she and Dad lived now, but she hadn't planted anything this year.

It got me through June, though, the smell of that dark earth coming up around my feet, shaking it out of the grass roots, my arms and back aching. I planted a whole row of rutabagas for Dad—he remembered growing huge rutabagas in that part of the field, and sometimes he could still eat the rutabagas Mom put in a stew for him. The deer took those first, pulling the tender greens out of the ground with gentle mouths, relishing the sweet root. We had put a small garden—lettuce and tomatoes and peas—in the clay-packed soil near the house, too. A back-up garden, just in case. Deer wouldn't come that close to the house, I thought, especially a house with Josh's *Metallica* coming from the windows. But by September, it was gone, too.

And there were elk—herds of elk, cows with calves, and heavy-antlered bulls. I'd never seen elk at the home place when I was growing up, but now we watched them every evening after supper from the kitchen window, crossing the clearing on the ridge above the house, blending into the red-brown brush on the other side. My brother John always saw them first, pointed with his chin the way I'd seen Dad do so many times, leaning against that same windowsill. John had moved in with us in late June, just after Father's Day, after he showed up in the same hospital with Dad. He had disappeared for three weeks. He'd lost his house by that time, and his car. When he followed his IV stand into Dad's room that morning, Dad decided that John should come stay at the ranch for a while. So he was with Dean and Josh and me, watching the deer, counting the elk.

"Let's drive up on the ridge," he said one evening. "Watch the elk come out on top." That was mid-July; he had been sober for twenty-seven days and our father was out of the hospital, back in his own bed at home. We did see the elk—three bulls, two big ones and a younger one—leap the barbed wire fence at the top of our place, from the timber into the midsummer hayfield. They lifted those big racks up into the last light, and then their red coats sank into dusk. By the time we drove back down the driveway, we were following our headlights through the dark.

Three days later my family would cross the hayfield on the upper ridge of the old home place, my oldest brother Tom lifting the wires for Mom to crawl through. Monte held the small black box of our father's ashes, his arms stiff against his belt buckle. A whitetail doe led her spotted fawn just ahead of us, looked back once, then leaped over the bank. The grass in the clearing was bent in the heat, yellow-white. Chunks of basalt poked through the grass. "He brought me here when we were first married," Mom said. "We looked out over the canyons and dreamed of building a house." When it was over we walked back along the old logging road, but I couldn't find the doe's tracks. John had gone down over the hill, startling the elk herd into blossom around him. They just lifted into the air like fawn-colored birds, he said. He was almost whispering. Then he disappeared for a week, and we finally told Mom yes, we'll go find him, we'll bring him home.

✤

I have a photograph of the deer hunters: the father and son team, blazing their red and orange against the pale yellow kitchen, hefting their rifles. They are clowning for the camera, because it's opening day and they feel excited and a little foolish. They don't know what they're doing. It's something you have to be taught. And nobody taught Dean—but he's the father, so here he is, at 3:30 in the morning (in the photo, the window is black), feeling like Elmer Fudd.

He had a plan, though. He and Josh had built a platform in a yellow pine at the edge of the new clearing my father had bulldozed out at the top of the ridge back when he thought he could escape his emphysema if he just kept moving. The clearing would be a place to park the travel trailer during the summer, up above the smoke of the canyon. It was rough terrain, ragged with cow parsley and fireweed now. But it might be a good place to be, Dean thought, at first light on opening morning.

And there was a back-up plan. If they hadn't seen anything by sunrise, he would bring the pickup back to the house; Josh would give him enough time to get home, then start down over the hill. Meanwhile, Dean and I would climb the east end of the hill and drive the brush thickets, pushing the deer toward Josh. He was carrying Dean's rifle, a .270 Winchester.

I remember the colors, the low brown brush and then the red of Josh's sweatshirt, watching him walk toward us. His eyes were blue-gray in this morning light, and he was looking, looking. *He's going to be okay*, I remember thinking.

Nothing had come toward Josh, so any deer on the hill must have gone down, hidden in the thicker brush between us and the field below. Together now, we pushed down the needle-slick ridge, parting the branches, listening. We had reached the road and had crawled through the fence into the field when I saw her. She stepped from behind the old-growth yellow pines Dad had left at the edge of the field, her front foot reaching like a delicate stem for the open space. "There!" It was my own voice, torn from me by surprise. The plan had worked: the deer was just where she should be. Dean and Josh raised their rifles, and she leaped into the field. *Go*, I told her. *Go*. I saw my father's rifle at the edge of my vision, shooting, then shooting again. She leaped, antelope-high, heading for the rockpile where the field dips down into woods, angled below the path of bullets. *Go*. Her side glimmered, still faintly summer red. Still whole, smooth. Another leap, she hung in the sky. Gone.

So maybe it was true, what Dean said later. You're driving them away, he said. They can sense it. How you feel.

But I think he was speaking for himself, too. He had shot other things, and he did not want to shoot a deer. Maybe he carried Dad's Winchester the way I carried the little saddle rifle: begrudging its weight, the focus it demanded as we crawled through a low trail under the brush.

I had no intention of using it.

On the way up the hill that first morning, I had heard his voice, shaking with the effort at silence. "If Josh gets a deer, I'm going to give him that .270," he said. That's what it was about, for both of us. Trying to make sure we didn't lose Josh that year, too. Something was happening to him that we didn't understand—something beyond the normal changes that come with starting high school. Last year he had wanted to learn to hunt. Maybe we could get him interested again, we thought—in hunting, in anything. John, of course, could have helped us. We could shoot, but we couldn't hunt. John could; Dad had made sure of that. But he was gone again. And it was just as well. Josh had sat in his shadow, watching, sharpening the knife his uncle had given him on a morning of remorse. His fingers wrapped around the neck of John's guitar, eyes closed as his other hand plucked silent music from the air above the strings. It's just the move, we told each other. He doesn't know anybody at school yet. And then losing his grandad like that. But at some level, even then, we knew.

He had made friends. We just didn't want to acknowledge them. How could those people be his friends? By this time, his teachers were telling us: something's wrong. He's with the wrong crowd. The drug crowd.

In my family we aren't very good at killing anything but ourselves, I thought as the season went on. Dean and I had struck a spark in our son that first morning—he was his old self, alert and excited, reaching up to touch Dean's shoulder on the walk back across the field, cupping his cold hands around the mug of hot chocolate in the kitchen, laughing through a brown mustache over the rim. But it didn't last. We scouted the hillside while he was in school, in the daylight—learning where the deer would be that afternoon, or that weekend—but Josh had lost interest. Once he missed the school bus, he said, and we watched him materialize through a cloud of gravel dust from a car full of senior girls yelling, "Tomorrow, Babe!" over a blaring tape deck. In the evenings he sat at the kitchen table, leaning into the telephone that propped his book open. Doing math homework, he said, with a girl named Storm. "I thought we could try the lower woods this Saturday, son," I heard Dean say as he poured himself another cup of coffee. "Look at *that*," Josh said, staring into the corner. Was he talking to Dean, or to Storm? "A giant rat just walked through the kitchen." He turned, looked over his shoulder at me. "Did you see that?" he said. "It was as big as a person!"

Still, we kept trying. I thought I knew that hillside, but I didn't. You learn the land by hunting it: I know that, now. You crawl up the little ravine, watching the pattern of shadows on rusted pine needles, tasting the earth in a way you don't, can't, unless you're hunting. You carry a burden, weighed to the earth by the line of that steel barrel. You listen. You can hear the white buckberries, like raindrops on the eave in full forenoon. And ravens, whispering overhead, steady as a heartbeat. I could walk that hillside now in the dark, find the deer trails through the thick brush like the way through a dream.

Which is what I was doing, really. There were October afternoons when the sun let me sit, just sit, against the yellowed grass, when the trees kept the secrets of those blue canyons behind them like a mother holding out her skirt, one hand behind her leg touching your head. 101 And once I heard the deer going through the brush below me, myself tangled in branches so thick I couldn't move. I heard a buck, too, stamping in the morning under the last of the starlight down in the draw, the day we got Josh up before dark to try to circle the lower woods before first light. And I heard the snow falling from the limbs overhead as we sat, back to back, listening to the light, a pheasant calling from the hill above us, a doe's back leg blending into bark. That was November, last summer's fern leaning and red now.

Between snows the earth came back, and I followed the old skid road around the hill to find Dad's ashes. I sat there a long time, waiting. Heavy morning fog pushed the blue canyon rims apart, all four of them, one behind the other until the river gave way to high Camas Prairie at the edge of my vision.

One morning, pushing through eight inches of new snow, I slid down into the bed a buck had just left, the black earth beneath a circle of fir branches, his dewclaws tracing a path at the edge of the snow as he'd leaped from earth to air. The snow lay smooth to the very edge of the ravine. I knew, then, why Dad had hunted this hill all those winters—without ammunition sometimes, he said—why he would come in blowing into his cupped hands, lean his cold rifle against the kitchen wall.

And I knew what it was to fly, to leap from sleep into life, to disappear. To keep breathing.

"Part of it, you know," Dean told me, "is just luck." We lay side by side in the dark bedroom. I could feel my breath pushing against the cold air.

On the last day we woke Josh before dark. We would climb the hillside just east of our hill and drive its brushy slope toward our land; Josh would be waiting in the timber just above the ravine. It had snowed again, nearly a foot this time, and the slope was steep. Dean broke trail for me, holding the vine maple branches until I was through the tight places. I touched his wool coat, just enough to feel its fur against my glove. Then we climbed higher.

But we were only halfway up the hill when he saw it. "What the—" he said, forgetting the hunter's vow of silence. I watched his eyes, reflecting his angle of vision, and then followed him around the face of the mountain until I could see it too: our son, wrapped in the bright pink blanket, leaning against a fir. His head was buried in the blanket.

"I don't think this is working," Dean said aloud.

It turned out to be one of those twenty-year winters, like the winter of '48 and the winter of '68. No matter how deep the snow got, though, there would be deer tracks just outside the kitchen door every morning. They were coming in to look for food, plum and apple twigs, or raspberry shoots. One night, coming home late from Mom's, we watched our headlights freeze three elk, their green eyes piercing the crabapple tree. The next morning I found their tracks, still there under the night's new snowfall, circling the house.

On the day before Christmas I went running, my shoes almost silent on the packed snow. Out where the road dipped over the canyon the morning sky looked like pink and orange scarves flung into the air, like a gypsy party without the music. I turned back, running into the mist of my own breath. Just below the old cemetery the road turned, and there he was—a fawn, white spots still bright against his coat. He looked at me and stepped toward me. Another step, then another. I was still running, moving slowly, like the current of last summer's drought-low river ebbing along over the rocky river bed. But he came steadily toward me as if I were a tree to shelter him: running now, tiny springs. Finally he leaped up, a balance of slender black hooves on the snowbank, and was gone into the darkness of the woods beyond.

We left in early January, struggling for an hour to get both rigs out of the driveway, and fought our way through the blizzard back to Oregon. Behind us two more feet of snow would fall, snowing-in the old place, and Mom's house in the valley too, for three days. We might have been able to raise a garden the next summer, because so many deer winterkilled. For a long time, even though I lived in town now, I looked down every time I stepped outside, looking for the circle of 103 tracks that would lift my eyes into morning.

# Salmon Run

It's like walking in armor. It's that thick, a scab over a wound, and when it lifts, like it does in the parking lot that evening, the pain makes me lightheaded. *No,* I whisper to the woman shouting at her son across the roof of their car. They have just come out of the DMV. The boy's voice wavers, frail against this flood, but she pours over him, waves of words. What has he done? "Never ... you couldn't even ... sick of it, you hear?" *Don't do it,* I will the woman through my icing windshield. She is pulling the car door open now, shaking the keys over the car roof. *You will regret these words, this righteous anger. This fat, mittened shaking.* I grip the steering wheel, my fingers yellowing with cold. I can't move. The woman settles herself in the driver's seat and the boy, tentative, slides in beside her. *Hush,* I tell her. *Look at his face, look at the back of his neck.* She backs out of the parking space, mouth wide, words still slicing over her shoulder. My fingers burn.

*If your child is alive and you know where he is, this is all that matters.* How could the woman hear me, even if I could say it? How could she remember it every minute of every day?

Besides, didn't I feel it too? This mother-anger? I try to remember. But the images come anyway, like the photos from all those albums, scenes that flash across the bedroom ceiling at night. "This will make those butterflies dance!" He's four, on his way out the door with an oatmeal box drum. He's dropping a clear plastic fishing float into the overflow creek at the foot of Ice Lake, the summer he was nine. There's a secret message inside, he says, for someone downstream to find. Now he's eleven, leaning forward from the backseat, his owl-feather voice brushing my ear. "All their personal things are intertwined," he sings. His voice will change in the fall, but it's still spring. His cheek feels like the thin sheets of water in the creek far below us, and his eyes are still blue-gray and clear.

I have to remember how to bend my fingers, how to shift. How to steer the car up the hill, toward home.

Sometimes breathing is the hardest part. I am so numb I forget how, I can't remember why. Sometimes—these are the worst times, and the easiest—I'm just angry, so angry I look at the faces of the men in my prison class who are up for murder and think: *my cousins, my kinsmen.* I understand the shapes of the penciled letters on their two allotted sheets of paper. These are the days when blame sprays in my wake like wood chips from the Potlatch chip trucks, blasting the windshield of anyone behind me, arcing out over the banks. It's all part of the same story, I think on those days. The juvenile officer with the nine-inch stack of case folders on his desk, the mental health counselors and hospital receptionists and Children's Services workers, the people who promised help and then said no, they couldn't give it, how had we possibly gotten the idea that they could? The treatment center that wouldn't let him back in because he had run away, the caseworker with the leather face on the other side of the table who told him, "You'll be out on the street in a few weeks and dead within a year. You might as well kill yourself and get it over with. Get out of our hair right now." "If there are no salmon to eat, let them eat something else," I hear Floyd Dominy of the Bureau of Reclamation say on television one night. The television documentary switches to black and white, the last dip-netting at Celilo, which the narrator mispronounces Ce-LEE-lo: "A vanishing fish for a vanishing race." *I promise you,* I had said to the leather-faced man, my voice shaking (how do these words sound to my son, sitting there in his too-short Juvie sweatpants and the ripped orange T-shirt? Does he see me looking for the mark on his neck?), *you think you don't care, but if he dies, I will make sure that you regret it, too.*

The angry days are the easiest, days when my hatred obliterates this chain of gray-white faces as if they were on TV with Floyd Dominy, click, off. Easiest because, of course, the face I really want to disappear is the one that startles me above the bathroom sink in the middle of the night and ambushes me from the blank glare of store windows. It is this face that my son turns to see, in the dream where the boy in the convertible is really him, his hair longer now but those are his ears, his shoulders—I am already reaching to touch his cheek—it is this face that makes his mouth twist into panic, shouting (his mouth dissolving like a smoke ring) to the driver, "Go! Go! Get out of here!" It is the face that, in refusing to let him die, has driven him away. *A hospital? A lockup hospital?* The face he is afraid of.

I would be different, I had told myself as a child. I would keep trying to hear the voices of the spirits that whispered in the pine needles. I would remember that grasses spoke, and ravens. April coyotes in the draw. I would live quietly, listening. When I grew up, there would be no more family quarrels, no more separation of mothers and sons.

But my son is gone. The voices I hear now are telling the story of Colonel Pratt and the boarding schools. A program on public television. *Kill the Indian and save the man.* I study the photograph of Pratt's supporters, the Friends of the Indian, gathered in the banquet hall to balance the savage force let loose by Sheridan, by Sherman and Custer. Their faces shine. I know a piece of something now that Colonel Pratt and the Friends of the Indian didn't learn: the price of good intentions.

He's been gone for almost two summers when Dean and I drive back up the highway to the lake where our son's life spark began. We want to sleep again in the mountains of Montana. A full moon follows us across the night, piercing my chest through the branches of the lodgepoles until I think no, this cannot be borne. At daybreak we follow the Going to the Sun highway over the backbone of the world and down into Browning. On the bench outside the general store a man waits to trade a stag-handled hunting knife for more wine. "Go on home now, Raymond," the clerk tells him. He leans over him, pointing up the street, but he doesn't touch him. "G'mornin'," the man says to us, putting the knife back into his pocket. He hunches his shoulders in his dirty nylon vest. The temperature has fallen forty degrees; behind us, in the mountains, two feet of snow cover the road.

"What's that *suyapo* doing here?" It's the old man's voice. The two Warm Springs men sitting on the bench beside me, a father and his grown son, look at me. "Don't listen to him." It's the father who speaks. His son nods. They are embarrassed. The father holds a single eagle feather; he will be one of the medicine singers tonight.

"It's all right," I tell them. I understand the old man's anger better than their forgiveness. The children have been stolen. And stolen again. How do you get over that? How can you forgive? The river too, of course. The salmon. The trees, the roots. Everything. Even these ceremonies were stolen, taken away by people whose hands couldn't hold them but took them anyway. The old man can remember when they had to hide behind blackout windows. People went to jail for dancing.

But one of my Indian students had waited after class to invite me here. "My mom wants you to come," she said. "It's a winter dance; it's for healing."

How does her mother know, I wonder? Or does everyone need healing? She had told her mother about me, Starla said. How I include Native writers in the class syllabus. I was so grateful that I could hardly listen to the directions, which Starla was drawing in purple ink. "It's right by the river," she said. "You'll find it. Everyone finds this place."

A woman on the bench behind me now touches my shoulder. An elder. "Come sit up here," she says. I squeeze in beside her. She is married to the man who called me *suyapo*, she says. She wants to know why I'm here. Then she tells me about another child, her daughter, who disappeared twenty-three years ago. Drinking, drugs. Twenty-three years. I can't look at her. We watch the young dancers in the tight circle, their dark hair leaping in the dim light as the room fills with sound.

It's like singing underwater, a chorus of light inside the darkness. These prayers, the elder tells me, are for everyone. For these young dancers, who are struggling right now. For her daughter. For my son, too.

Long after I've forgotten about time, the dancing stops. "Thank you," I say to Starla's mother, Lucinda. "Thank you for inviting me." Tomorrow is my son's birthday, I tell her. The second since he's been gone. "These songs—"

"Tell them," she says. She rings a small bell, and the voices stop. "This is Starla's teacher," she says. "She has something to tell you." I hear my voice, words small as pine needles, floating above the silence of the room. *My son seventeen gone and.... this healing, for him and.... for me.... thank you.*

107

❧

"You live with it," Lucinda tells me. I don't understand it, but I too just keep breathing. In and out. Like the two little boys she cares for, who watched as their father followed their mother into the bedroom, holding the knife. "I told that social worker," she says. "I'm not real educated, but I don't think they need to be sticking pins into balloons. They know what happened. We talked about it."

By now I know her house by the river. The door is never locked, and if she finds me waiting on the steps, my fingers deep in the neck fur of the old dog, Lucinda wonders why I haven't just gone inside. It's a rough board house like the one I grew up in. But this is the house that Lucinda's father had pulled down from the Japanese Internment Camp in the hills just above us after The Dalles Dam flooded Celilo Falls and he had to find a place for his family to live. Two barrack sections, joined together.

How does it feel to hear the floodgates close, to watch the water behind the big new wall of concrete smothering Celilo? You have ridden out over white froth in a swinging cable car with the gorge wind pushing spray into your face, sharing the ride back to the women waiting on the river bank with a salmon almost as big as you are. Your father and his father, and his, have heard the river roaring a circle around their dreams on Big Island for longer than you can imagine. For fourteen thousand years Celilo has been the center of life, the heart of culture in the Northwest. The point of balance between men's roles and women's, between people and animals, water and fire. I think of London, casually flooded. Or Rome, becoming Atlantis. I try to imagine leaving the river that day. When the swallows flew upriver next spring, who would be there to greet them? Who would know their language? Not even a grandmother will be able to keep you from the Catholic boarding school at Warm Springs, where you will be Number 25 in the morning line to use the bathroom.

The voices that gather around Lucinda's long table are quiet. Sometimes there is laughter, often silence. Always, outside, I can hear the river. On Sunday morning there is a dish of roots cooked with salmon that I hold inside my mouth, savoring the taste for a long time

108

before I swallow. I remember the Ice Age story of the fight between the wolves and the salmon, eternal ice and the flow of the seasons. The wolves destroy all the salmon, even all of the salmon eggs: all but one, small and shriveled, stuck in a crack of rock too deep for their licking tongues. This one is washed out by the spring rains, slips downriver to the grandmother who waits to nurture him, teach him, send him back ...

Little swimmer. I remember my son's small, slick body, his underwater smile. I remember pushing him up for a breath of air.

Fewer and fewer salmon are making it past the dams this year. One man shakes his head. "Yeah, they gotta have their power." It's a bitter joke. Just past the serviceberry bush, at the edge of the still-swift Deschutes, is the sweat house. Another kind of power.

When the meal is over, it ends as it has begun, with water. "*Chuus.*" Everyone pushes back from the table.

I speak his name aloud, sometimes, as if it will keep him alive. *Josh. Joshua.* People blink, turn away. "It would be easier if you knew he was dead," they say. One woman urges me to have a laying-to-rest ceremony for him.

When the army followed the Navajos into Canyon de Chelley, I remember reading, some escaped capture and the long walk south to the killing place, the concentration camp at Bosque Redondo. Every day these people climbed the hills and spoke the names of the missing ones aloud. Four years later, some of them—the ones left alive—came home.

On PBS, they're talking about the rivers again. Floyd Dominy says he's sorry they didn't dam every river. All that wasted power! David Brower, who stopped the avalanche of dams and even the dam in the center of the Grand Canyon, believes he's a failure because he didn't stop the Glen Canyon dam. A woman begins to cry. She had looked up at the cathedral rock formation, she says, from the bottom of Glen Canyon; in her boat on the dam's reservoir later, she would look down at a faint glint in the water and realize it was the cathedral, buried, still catching the light.

109

But the Glen Canyon dam, another old river runner reminds us, will eventually disappear. Like the other sixteen basalt-flow dams that have plugged the Canyon. See? You can read it in the canyon walls. One by one, these stone dams have cracked under the river's need to flow. Vanished.

It just takes time, he says.

How many salmon make it back up the river? I understand the odds. It has been two years now. But he's not dead. I can feel him, under my heart. I will know, I tell myself, if he dies. And he comes to me, now, in dreams. His skin is incredibly warm, his voice softened by love. "I need to stay here a while longer," he tells me.

One morning I wake just at sunrise with the light from my dream spreading into the curtain and the dew-whitened grass of the back yard. I have seen the sacred earth, lit from within, a golden light. The arched bodies of gods, long and narrow like Rainbow God, held up the hills. "All the earth is sacred," said the voice beside me, inside me. "Here, they can see the gods in the earth because they know this. But it's sacred where you stand, too."

The dream stays with me, floating behind my eyes. I'm walking beside the North Fork—just a narrow creek now in the August heat—when I see them. They arch, splashing the shallow water into the sun. Spring chinook: silver and black, their bodies scarred and torn. Their battered heads turn upstream, into the current. The male chases a trout as it darts from the bank, eager for a taste of her eggs.

There's a lot of talk now about breaching the dams, digging channels to let the river flow around them. Even removing some dams, the ones upstream. We'll have to decide, other people say. The cost, they add, might be too high. After all, it's just a fish.

Meantime, against all odds, a few salmon batter their way through. I watch the water, waiting. You have to be ready to welcome them, I know, or they will quit coming back to us forever.

# Homeless

The first summer our son was missing was also the first summer that the Wallowa Valley Band of the Nez Perce, the descendants of Chief Joseph's people, came back to the high mountain valley to dance the summer dances. The people of Wallowa called it the First Annual Friendship Feast and Powwow, and they invited the Ni Mii Pu to use the high school gym. Maybe they were just trying to save their town now that the mill was closing. They were honest about that side of things. But no matter how hard times were, nobody had ever done this before. It wasn't that people weren't ashamed of what had happened here. Even General Howard had known it was wrong. But when Joseph made a trip back to the valley years after the war—and imprisonment and exile and trips to Washington to plead for his people's survival— to buy a ranch for his people to live on, one hundred and sixty acres of the sacred place where the fathers' and mothers' bones lay buried, no one would sell to him. How do we begin to heal a wound this deep? In Wallowa, they simply put the coffee on and opened the door.

We had to go. Driving down the Minam grade, Dean said he could hear the drums again, not the drums from the powwow ahead but the ones you can hear coming up from the canyon below you, like your own heart. He said he had heard them the first time we ever drove down this mountain, too. Outside the gym people were selling fry bread and sno-cones, and a man looked up as a golden eagle circled over our heads. "A good sign!" he told us. Inside they were having a giveaway, part of the naming ceremony. A woman filled my arms with white and blue skeins of yarn. Then the drums wrapped around me, behind me and over and over as the dancing began. Another woman came to sit next to us on the bottom bleacher row. "That's my son," she told Dean. A man circled by us, holding a baby in his arms. "There's his wife. He made those leggings. They're all going back to tradition now." I held the yarn against my chest. Traditional dancers and grass dancers and jingle dancers and fancy dancers. Men and women and children circled around and around. For the first time I forgot to count the days.

What is home? I thought a lot about this during the time our son was missing. I knew he didn't have one, and although we had a place to lay our heads and a mailbox in our new town, I didn't feel like we had one either. I kept thinking of that Walt Whitman poem about the spider casting its filament out into the universe. If that gossamer thread you fling out doesn't catch somewhere (o my soul), where are you? What are you standing on?

But Josh had gone home, we heard. He'd gone right back to Joseph, the little town below Wallowa Lake where we had lived for eleven years until, ten days before he would graduate from eighth grade, a tax levy failed and my teaching position was eliminated. If he hadn't been uprooted at that dangerous, transitional time ... if the Wallowa Valley were still home? That June when we moved back to the home place above the Clearwater River for a few months, we were coming home to help as my father's illness led him closer to his death, but coming home too as if by instinct—that's where you go when you're lost. And that was the second place we found traces of Josh. When he'd been missing for three weeks, we got a call: he was found, he was safe, being held in Clearwater, Idaho. We hugged each other, we cried. "I'm probably the only person in Oregon who knows there *is* such a place as Clearwater, Idaho!" I said. But even as I said it, I knew something was wrong. Where would they be "holding" him in Clearwater, a tiny village up the South Fork, not much more than an old building? It turned out to be a garbled message—the sheriff of Clearwater County had only said yes, he was sure he'd seen him.

And then Josh was gone with no tracks left to follow. The phone calls and letters to his old friends, those hours we spent climbing over the rocks at the foot of Wallowa Lake and driving up and down and streets of Joseph and Orofino, gave us nothing. There were false leads we clung to like desperate dreamers clutching at clouds to break their fall—"Yeah, he was here in Pendleton last week; I saw him at the Mini-Mart"—even when we knew better. We watched the red light of the answering machine as if it were a beacon. Sometimes the phone rang and no one answered. "I love you," I said into the silence. "Please come home." Once a young voice woke us at three in the morning: "Dad? I need to come home. Can you come get me?" But it was the wrong voice, someone else's boy. That winter a W-2 slip arrived. Josh had worked for a few days picking fruit in Mattawa, Washington. He was Colin Aaron Lynch now. His middle name, his cousin's name, and my family name. That was something, wasn't it? Couldn't we cling to that? And he'd listed us as his home address. But the phone call led nowhere. No, they didn't know where he had gone, left with some woman, the man said. He didn't know her name. I remembered the newspaper articles about Mattawa and the fruit-pickers' camps along the river, the pitiful conditions where families lived under tarps.

I saw him everywhere. Places he'd never go—the flea market, softball games in the park. He was running down the hill below the Forest Service offices, flipping back his hair in Albertsons. Once I followed a woman in a yellow Wagoneer up the South Hill until she pulled into her driveway and got out, looking back over her shoulder at me. A middle-aged woman, starting to unload her groceries. So maybe seeing him standing by the freeway entrance ramp with a dirty pack, or dragging a black plastic bag along the river levee, was not so unusual. I stared into the faces of these men, searching for my son behind their shadows. Men of all ages drifted down from the freeway, looking, looking everywhere but at me. Sometimes they would catch my face meeting theirs and freeze. Men with long hair, men with mustaches, men with tattoos and dark eyes. Migrants shouting their anger in other languages. Young men, boys really, bare chested in the park, heading for the levee. Carloads of heads, turning to look back at me.

Pendleton's bag lady didn't notice me, though. She knew who she was looking for. I'd see her walking up Emigrant Avenue with her three shopping bags, always dressed in her blue coat, leaning down sometimes to shade her eyes and peer into parked cars or the glaring windows of empty storefronts. She was on her way to the freeway off-ramp, where she would stay as long as the light lasted, sitting on a guardrail post with her small plastic bags around her feet. She was waiting, the kids from Mission told me, for her son. He had left her here years ago. Maybe she had watched him disappear over the skyline where the freeway climbs Reith Ridge and drops into the desert. She

113

was waiting for him to come back for her. The kids keep an eye on things. They listen to the way people laugh or don't laugh. They hear the stories of their reservation and Pendleton too. She's rich, one girl said. She's got a great big house. But she sleeps under the bridge; no, said another, she's got a room in that place down by the lumberyard, you know where the sign hangs on one hinge, where the street gets real narrow? Day after day I passed the woman sitting by the off-ramp. Her dark face wrinkled against the wind. The streets rose up alphabetically around us, climbing the hills on both sides of the river valley up to the wheat fields where the sky takes over, piling up its thunderheads all the way to the Blues. Byers, Carden, DeSpain, Furnish, Goodwin, all the leading families of the Historical Society. I didn't know her name. *Sister,* I thought.

I knew something now that I had only guessed the day I met the homeless vet in the laundromat. It was twenty below zero that day, early January. We had just come back to Oregon so I could teach part time at the community college in Pendleton. Josh's bedroom was at the other end of the empty trailer we had rented—we had our beds and clothing and a few dishes but everything else was still waiting to be retrieved over the snow-drifted road from Idaho—and when I walked down the hall to the bathroom at night I listened to the silence. Was he there? Sometimes I stepped inside and tried to make my eyes focus in the dark. I couldn't hear him breathing, and I was afraid to turn on the bedroom light. He kept his clothes packed in a suitcase in the middle of the bedroom floor. He was fourteen.

That morning, though, I was sure he had climbed on the bus headed for school and I was getting ready for class, trying to learn all about George Orwell before my 11 o'clock, "Down and Out in Paris and London," reading alone in the laundromat while the clothes tumbled, when a man in a mackinaw came in the front door. I watched him pace along the row of dryers, feeling inside the drums. He read the instruction sign hanging above the tuna-can ashtray. He was wearing a navy watch cap and insulated lace-up boots. His backpack leaned against the bench by the door.

"I came in here to dry out my sleeping bag," he said, grinning at me as if we'd been talking all the while. "Gotta be sure to keep it dry." He peered at the sign again. "How long do these dryers run for a quarter, you know?"

"About five minutes, I think," I said.

"Oh." He lifted the bag from his pack and held it against his chest. "I've got a down bag," he said, "good for twenty below. If it gets colder than that, I'm in trouble. But I was okay last night." He walked over to the row of dryers again. I looked down at George Orwell. The man was in the laundromat to get warm, I knew.

"You know anybody going to Walla Walla today?" He came over and stood by the row of washers I was using, keeping the white machines between us. I shook my head. "I just need to be sure I get there. How far is it?"

"Forty-five miles or so, I think."

"I don't want to get stranded on that road," he said. "Day like today, I might not make it. Usually I'd just hitch, but day like today a guy's gotta be careful. I'm going over to the VA hospital there. You been there?"

"Yes," I told him.

"See, I've got a card. You know how they give you a card?" He set the sleeping bag on top of the washer and stepped around the machines, pulling a wallet from inside his coat. "I can get in, if I can just get over there." He held out a metal ID card. The raised letters said HOMELESS VET. "There's no address, but they put "homeless vet" right on there, and they let me in," he said. "But I gotta be sure I get there. Pretty cold. I didn't expect it to be so cold here." He looked back at the dryers. "I've just gotta be careful," he said. "But I do pretty good. I got these insulated boots." He held up one foot, showing me. "And that bag is a good one. I oughta put it through the dryer." He unbuttoned his coat and pulled a cigarette from his shirt pocket, cupping his hand around the match.

115

"Bag got me through last night," he said, leaning against the washer again. "I come in on the train, knew I could get a night in detox and stay warm. I had a bottle and drank most of it and headed for detox, but they said they moved it. Clear to the other end of town, out by the prison. That's five miles, and I wasn't in shape to walk that far. Did you know they moved detox?"

"I know where it is now," I said.

"It used to be in the hospital," he said. "So I had to sleep under the bridge. I'm all right long as it don't get below twenty below. I got a little stove and I can make hot water, drink some tea before I get out of the bag, then I'm okay." He smoked. "Some people, though," he said. "They just don't know. Couple women went by this morning while I was heating my water, looked up and saw me there under the overpass, and they just laughed and waved."

I shook my head. "You have quarters? I have an extra quarter," I told him.

"Naw. It don't need it, really. It's a good bag," he said. He picked it up and tucked it under one arm. "I'm going back out now, see if I can hitch a ride. I can come back in here and warm up every little bit."

I watched him walk to the edge of the highway that would start its climb up the ridge just beyond the view from the laundromat window. Then I looked down at the book in my lap. I had to make this job work. When I looked up, he was gone.

Josh was three the summer that I had heard about the teaching job in Joseph and thought the Wallowa Valley, leaning up against the Eagle Cap Wilderness, would be the perfect place for a boy to grow. I suppose it was as close as I could come to actually going home, although it was across Hell's Canyon from the Clearwater drainage. In fact, I had picked out this valley years before, the year I was twelve. Since I couldn't live on the ranch in Idaho when I grew up—I was a girl with three brothers, and the rules of gender seemed clear—the only other place I thought I belonged was in Joseph. I had not seen it then, just read the stories.

Now that we had lost our home there, signing a quit-claim deed to the little house that looked out on the mountain, I wondered how I could ever have promised to make payments on even fifty feet of this land that I knew should still belong to the Nez Perce. Dean and I had agreed that we were living in Joseph as temporary guests. If the old Nez Perce treaties are ever enforced—twice, before they were driven out, the Wallowa Valley Band had been assured that this valley was reserved for them—we would leave this little house behind us.

116

Wherever we stop our wagons and unpack the cooking kettles is somebody's sacred place, I told myself. Thank you, thank you, I had whispered every morning, running along between the glacial moraine and the lake as the stars faded and the sun rose over the moraine to touch the big mountain that whites had named for Chief Joseph. I loved the mule deer tracks in the winter streets, the way we could smell a big snow coming down Hurricane Creek, the roar of the river out of Wallowa Lake. But I knew there was much wrong. There were no Indians, no dark skins of any kind. Once, watching Josh and his friend Skywalker playing on the rocks near the foot of the lake, I had looked down to see a red arrowpoint shining just beneath the water.

It felt awful to lose my job. I hadn't seen it coming; in a startling fifteen minutes, I belonged nowhere. If a teacher loses her job, she does not fit into another slot in the community. When we walked down to Bud's Hardware to buy supplies to build a moving rack for our pickup, I felt embarrassed, as if we were being evicted by the town itself. Is this how the Ni Mii Pu felt, I wondered? Thirty days to round up your stock and pack up your lives and get out? And then, of course, I felt guilty for the thought. We had lived in Joseph for eleven years, not eleven thousand.

When Josh was gone I read and re-read the story of the event that had precipitated the Nez Perces' being ordered to the reservation at Lapwai. White families newly settled in the adjacent Grande Ronde Valley had come into the Wallowa River drainage to find pastures for their cattle in 1872. By now a surveyor had marked out the Wallowa Valley in grids, and many families struggling with respiratory illnesses on the coastal side of Oregon had been told that both of these high, drier valleys were now "open" for homesteading. Lawyer, head man of the band at Lapwai, had signed the 1863 treaty reducing the Nez Perce reservation (but preserving his own people's lands) and despite Joseph's famous analogy—how can another man sell you my horses?—it was convenient for Congress to believe that Lawyer had signed for all the Nez Perce people. The settlers came right past Old Joseph's deadline of lodgepoles surrounded by rock piles three or four feet high which he had erected above the Minam River to mark the Nez Perce boundary. It wasn't easy. They had to take the wagons apart and lower them in

117

pieces over Smith Mountain. Alexander and Sarah Findley's family
were among the first to arrive. They built a cabin near the junction of
the Wallowa and Lostine rivers, only a half mile from where the Ni
Mii Pu held their summer encampment. The next year President Grant
issued an executive order protecting the valley from settlement, but
people kept coming anyway. Joseph often came by the Findleys for
dinner. He played with their children. The Findleys considered him
their friend.

How much land do you need? Joseph asked at one point in his
patient and firm efforts to preserve his people's land. If every family
needs only a hundred and sixty acres, there is room for us all here. It
was the open-range grazing that caused problems for both whites and
Indians. Stock trampled gardens. Horses went missing. When Findley
couldn't find five of his horses, he enlisted the help of a young,
hotheaded neighbor named McNall and went looking for them. There
are several stories about what happened next. It sounds like they rode
into a Nez Perce hunting camp and accused the Indians of stealing the
horses—and McNall wrestled over a rifle with Wilhautyah, Wind
Blowing. "Shoot him! Shoot him!" he yelled. As the struggle went on
he began to weaken; he was screaming curses at Findley. Then his rifle
went off and Findley thought his neighbor had been shot. At the same
instant, he said later, Wilhautyah reached for the rifle and even though
it was now empty, Findley was afraid. So it was he who fired the killing
shot. Three days later he found his horses grazing quietly near his
cabin, and within the year the Ni Mii Pu would be gone.

There had been no retaliation, only insistence on justice. At one
point Wilhautyah's daughter came to the door, looked at Findley, and
turned away silently. Findley, shaken, wanted to go with the Nez Perce
people to accept their judgment, but other settlers restrained him.
Finally there was a hearing—but only for Findley, not McNall. Findley
had acted in self-defense, said the judge. He requested another hearing
by a grand jury, but again he was held blameless. In the months after
the killing, when Joseph was trying hard to fend off the agents and
military men from Lapwai and Walla Walla who wanted to resolve
these problems by removing the Ni Mii Pu from the valley, he visited
the Findleys again. He let their oldest daughter ride his horse, and
gave her a shell earring.

118

Alexander Findley put the rifle away and never fired it again. But in 1878—by then Joseph's people were imprisoned in Kansas, and he had lost all his children but one, a twelve-year-old daughter in Canada he would never see again—the Bannocks to the southeast of Joseph rose up to fight for their survival, and when the white people of the Grande Ronde and Wallowa valleys gathered to protect themselves in case the Indians came that far east, a diphtheria epidemic broke out. Half of the children in the Grande Ronde Valley died, and the Wallowa Valley was hit hard too. The Findleys lost six of their seven children. Only Florence, the girl with the shell earring, survived. That winter when Findley took his cattle down to Joseph Canyon to winter them, Sarah came along. Although it was the woman's winter job to keep up the homestead chores in addition to her own, Sarah could not stay there without him now. Their last child would be born in a cave along Joseph Creek, perhaps the same cave where Chief Joseph had been born. Then a spark caught their cabin on fire. The only thing that they found in the ashes was the can of buttons Sarah had saved, Joseph's shell earring safe among them. They would leave the valley a broken family.

The first year Josh was gone we watched the phone as if it were alive. He would call on Thanksgiving. On Christmas, surely. On his birthday: he'd be eighteen, the laws of juvenile runaway behind him now. He'd leave a message: Hey this is Josh, just wanted to let you guys know I'm okay. I remembered the sound of his voice that time when he had disappeared for two weeks, *got some things to take care of, don't worry about me.* But this time he didn't call. Was he alive? Was he really so angry or scared that we would never see him again—until he was thirty, maybe forty, maybe never? I remembered his face, how it lit when he saw us 119 the night that the jailer in Weiser had called; he's run away from the treatment center but he's turned himself in two hundred miles down the road, come take him home. Always, no matter how desperately he had struggled against our frantic efforts to make him stop using, he had loved us. But he had plenty to run away from. The troubles of our little family, our mistakes and craziness and our desperate willingness to do anything to make our son safe, even call the police, played like heavy metal tapes in my head, discordant and jarring.

How could things have gone so wrong? I had taught high school long enough to know that almost all kids do some adolescent drinking and many experiment with drugs, too. But most of them get through it. Most of them sleep in their own beds every night, and graduate. Our story was more complicated, I knew. Dean and I had been living with the ravages of his post-traumatic stress disorder since before our son was born, and the medication that would later free us from the fear and rage that could come unexplained out of the bluest skies was yet to be discovered. All it takes, we had thought as young parents, is love. We love each other, and we love our child. We understand what a gift he is. Being the spring that nurtures his growth is the most important thing, the purpose of our lives. Love, we thought, was the way to heal any wound. But our years of struggle, trying to keep upright in this storm, sometimes pushed all three of us beyond the boundaries that had held us through Josh's childhood. When he was eleven we found him passed out in the garage, his breath heavy with gasoline. The next few years would be full of counselors and denial and then juvenile officers and lockups—and growing insanity on our part as we tried frantically to pull our boy back into his life and he pulled further and further away. By the time he was fifteen he had gone from being a "talented and gifted" student to one who had failed most of his freshman classes and been refused admission even to the alternative school because he'd run away from treatment so many times. "You're killing your mother—can't you see that?" I heard Dean say one afternoon, his voice cracked and splintering. "I brought you into this world, I can take you out of it!" What had we come to?

Sometimes, washing the dishes or holding a pencil, I looked at my hands and wondered how they could have become so scarred, so weathered, and yet have been so weak and clumsy, powerless to keep my own child safe, to wipe that look from his face (dirty face—and—as if by magic—clean face!), to lift him into my arms, lift him out of this. Once I stood at the top of our driveway in a late-summer rain with my arms locked around his waist, trying to hold him back. Dean had rescued him from the street at three a.m. the night before and sat with his arm around his shoulders urging him to eat something, anything—but after a night's sleep Josh was returning to what he called his "street family." To break my hold he would have to hurt me, though, and he wouldn't do it. I was pleading, tomorrow is the first day of school, please, please, I was stacking the good things on a balance scale inside my heart like so many weightless feathers. Fishing, camping, how many hours of swimming, since he was only four months old, slippery on his father's shoulders, laughing? Riding bikes—remember his little one? Catching crawdads, backpacking. Laurel and Hardy and popcorn, his giggle in the theater darkness, reading, reading, even at the end, *The Milagro Beanfield War*, taking turns; the only parents to attend all the pee wee baseball games, those soccer games, feathers, feathers. Watching him carry in the flag at the Cub Scout meeting, the 4-H photography club, and the log cabin Dean helped him build in the back yard. Saturday morning chocolate waffles. Music filling the house. The road trips, our voices in the truck: "In a couple of years they have built a home, sweet home / with a couple of kids running in the yard of Desmond and Molly Jones." None of it would stop this downhill pull.

Near the end of the first summer Josh was gone, Dean bought a motorcycle. "Ride with me," he said. I swung my leg over the seat behind him because it didn't really matter now, anyway. The helmet came down over my face and smothered my breathing, and as we climbed the curving grade up to the high desert I could feel myself sailing off into the waiting canyon. But maybe that was just the sensation of falling I carried inside me all the time. By the time we reached the tall pines at Battle Mountain, I had felt the earth like a blanket beneath us, and on the way back down the grade its pulsing songs pushed under the face shield and into my ears. I could hear the land again, this arrowroot balsam hillside of rock and sunlight, talking to me like the home place above the Clearwater did. There were stories in this earth. Lives whispered from the yellow grasses. For the first time since he'd been gone I felt part of something larger, something whole.

So we rode. "Already you have passed me on my road," a line from the Zuni creation story, kept singing in my head. But the elderberries and apples ripened into October gold along the Umatilla, and when the kingfisher rose up with his beak full of trout I could see Josh standing in the same spot, the flick of his cast. Herons lifted out of the current and into the air above the river, too heavy for their miracle of flight. *We share the earth,* I knew, letting myself float into this ride. *He's somewhere on this earth, or in it. We're part of it together.* I remembered the heron poem he had written the autumn he was eight, his eyes the color of the heron's feathers. Dean and I put on insulated coveralls and rode on Christmas Day. Everyone thought we were crazy.

The call came on June 18, 1993. It had been two years and eight days. It was nine o'clock, and we were watching the Apache story from a series of videotapes called *How the West Was Lost.* I was thinking about Geronimo's vision, the way he stared straight at the camera, when the phone rang. He's here, a woman said. He's in the police station in Bunker Hill, Illinois, waiting for a ride home. They'd been stopped, he and a friend, for riding a motorcycle without eye protection. No, he didn't know about the missing person's report, he didn't know I was on the line. Would I like to talk to him?

My God, My God. "I love you, don't hang up, are you there?" It was a miracle on the end of a filament; like when he was small and we went fishing with a two pound test line ... "We have a motorcycle, too!" (How can I tell him: listen, don't hang up? Things are different now?) I was crying and laughing. We'll be on the next plane, I told him. We have to see you. His voice, soft and confused and joyful in my ear: "We don't have a place of our own," he was saying. "We're just living with other people."

Then we are looking down at the Rockies, at Green River. The endless plains. We're traveling on invisible lines in the sky. There are webs that catch us, weave us into their mysteries. Below us is the same land my grandmother walked across when she was seven and eight years old, and I am retracing her steps, and Josh did too; we are circling around and around on this land. Then the plane was dipping toward that strange arch above the brown river, and we were running down the ramp into the St. Louis airport and a circle of arms, father's and mother's and child's. He looked like a very thin Mark Twain, his hair sun-bleached and parted in the middle. I smelled his neck, his hair. People hurried past us, coming in and flying out, black bags bumping along toward their own Father's Day reunions. We couldn't let go of him. "I still drink and smoke a little, but I don't do the hard stuff any more, Mom," he had said into the phone. "It's all right, it's all right, I just love you," I had told him. There was a long way to go, I knew, but it felt like we were already there, like I was the mother spider with the filament centered in all my arms, ready for the stories that would spin out in any direction.

# Learning to Live on Stolen Land

# On Water and On Land

It's a warm April afternoon, with the long light of evening already coming across the hills above the water. Josh is behind me in the inflatable canoe, pushing us across the lake with the kayak-style paddle. When I look over my shoulder at him, he grins. For a moment I remember him at five, sliding on the seat of his pants down the steep trail from Maxwell Lake and using a stick as a kayak paddle, his face bright with pretending the trail is a whitewater chute, dust and small rocks flying. We glide closer to a pair of mallards and I trail my fingers in the cool water. We are in the water and on it, suspended between the elements. "Magic," I say. "Of course, you're doing all the work."

"It's not much work," he says. "With only one person in it, it's even easier. Effortless." Then his face tightens with sudden worry. "I don't know what I was thinking of—I should have let you try it alone."

"Couldn't get much better than this," I tell him. He's pushing us closer and closer to the cottonwoods submerged in the high waters of this spring's snowmelt. Then we are in them, sunlight falling in patches around us. Josh steers us around submerged branches and windfalls, back paddles. Then, not three feet above my head, a flicker emerges from the round hole of a cottonwood. He looks at us for a long moment, that bright red streak painting a line above his black bib and the intricate mosaic beneath it. We hold perfectly still. And then he is gone, a flash of orange and brown, his flight nearly silent.

We poke around in the watery woods—I'm pretending it's the Everglades, but I don't say so. Something is making a mighty flopping sound beyond the willows; we're pretty sure it's carp but it might be a beaver. Josh tells me he has paddled right up to them, pushing the canoe through the inlet at the other end of the lake on his fishing expeditions. "Wow," I whisper. "That must be quite a feeling."

"It is," he says. "And a little bit scary, too, being eye to eye with a beaver all of a sudden. This one was big—huge. 'Don't bite the canoe!' I kept thinking." We laugh. The flickers have made several trips to the

127

nest hole, ignoring this new two-headed beaver moving slowly through their world, by the time we find the carp. It's getting cool, too, the last of the sun hitting the tops of the cottonwoods, and a breeze is beginning to lift the lake into ripples. Josh paddles us quickly across the water now. "Don't worry," he says. "This canoe will handle waves. That time Tom and I got caught in that storm out on Thief Valley Reservoir we were both pretty scared—we'd left the life jackets in the truck (I know, I know! Haven't don't that since, though ...). Two-foot waves, at least, but this canoe just pushed through them. We were clear out in the middle, too." I shiver. "Got pretty cold by the time we made it in, but I'm kind of glad it happened. I trust this canoe now. It's amazing. I'd like to take it out in the ocean and see how it does."

The Cabela's catalog didn't describe this little craft as an ocean-going vessel, but I don't say anything. These waves don't amount to much, and we're on shore before I know it. He wants me to try the canoe solo to see how much easier it steers. I thrash around in circles a few yards off the bank, laughing. "Took me a while to get the hang of it," he says into the growing dusk. But it's going to take me longer, I can tell. And it's cold in this breeze with the sun gone. We pull the canoe out and deflate it. "Thanks," I tell him. My hand is on his shoulder as he kneels, folding the canoe to fit in the trunk. "A perfect birthday. Thank you, Josh."

"It's not much," he says. "Should've done it a long time ago."

For the two years that Josh was missing, I thought *if I could know he's alive, somewhere, that would be enough.* I wouldn't have to know where. I wouldn't have to see him again.

Such silent bargains I made with God.

128 The truth is so much better than I dared to imagine. Josh lives in Oregon again, just across the valley from our house. Healing works its way out from the center after the surface wound has closed, and it takes time, maybe longer than any of us have in one lifetime. But who could have expected a chance like this? We can talk to each other. We can say we're sorry. He can call us: "You guys all right in this wind?" We can share a pizza, a favorite fishing spot. He shows me where the

morels are growing this year, and the good huckleberry patches. Sometimes we hike up to the high lakes, the way we did every summer when he was a kid, just the two of us. Grateful isn't a big enough word. Maybe another language has a word that could wrap its way around the way I feel when I look at my son, or hear his laugh, or watch him feinting and dodging, playing tag in the back yard with his dog.

Every time he says good-bye—on the phone, or waving from his truck window, or calling across the parking lot if I've stopped by the Chevron station where he works—he says, "I love you." He says it the way other people say "see you later."

But the truth is, as grateful as I am, I want more. I want him to find peace, the happiness of being completely himself, everything he is and can be—and to keep growing, always growing into the self he is becoming. I want him to reach beyond the limitations of the story he grew up in.

Above my desk is a poster I made for my American Literature class. I used a photo that I took years ago, my dad walking hand in hand with Josh down a rain-puddled road. Josh is less than two, reaching out ahead of him with a "walking stick." Dad's hair is graying under his black felt crusher, and he's slowing his steps to match his grandson's. I made the poster as a gift to my students, an invitation to the journey we would be taking as a class. But as I look at it now, I realize that it was really for Josh all along. All of it: the photograph, the lines from Whitman's poem that rise out of the picture, all these words I try to pass along.

*I tramp a perpetual journey.*
*My signs are a rain-proof coat and good shoes, and a staff cut from the*
  *woods.*
*No friend of mine takes his ease in my chair.*
*I have no chair, nor church, nor philosophy;*
*I lead no man to dinner-table or library or exchange,*
*But each man and woman of you I lead upon a knoll.*
*My left hand hooks you round the waist,*
*My right hand points to landscapes or continents, and a plain public road.*

*Not I, not any one else, can travel that road for you.*
*You must travel it for yourself.*

*It's not far ... it is within reach,*
*Perhaps you have been on it since you were born, and did not know,*
*Perhaps it is every where on water and on land.*

*Shoulder your duds, dear son, and I will mine, and let us hasten forth ...*

*Long have you timidly waded, holding a plank by the shore,*
*Now I will you to be a bold swimmer,*
*To jump off in the midst of the sea, and rise again and nod to me and shout,*
*   and laughingly dash with your hair ...*

Perhaps it *is* everywhere, on water and on land. But if my family is going to escape the story we have found ourselves trapped inside, we will have to learn to see it. We'll have to learn to look at the world and each other with a different vision, until every place is a home place.

Where to begin? If I could wrap it up and give it to my son like a sacred bundle, what would it look like?

"What are you *looking* at over there, every morning?" The man had to raise his voice a little above the sound of his engine, and he was smiling, a little embarrassed. He had waited while I put down the binoculars and leaned over from the passenger side of my car to roll down the driver's side window.

I leaned a bit lower and craned my neck to see him, high in his extended-cab white Ford. "Oh, just birds," I tossed up, an initial offering. It wasn't exactly a secret, what I was really doing, but I had to be careful not to share it with just everyone. He wasn't buying the bird-watching story, though, I could tell. Who'd be parked in this same pulloff at the foot of the hill before sunrise all summer long? "And there's a den of foxes over on that hillside. I like to watch the little foxes." Now my grin was as sheepish as his.

"Oh," he said. He was trying to imagine such a thing. Getting up every morning at the crack of dawn to stare across a pasture and through a maze of cottonwoods along the creek over there, hoping to catch a

130

glimpse of—fox? *Should foxes be shot?* I felt a lurch of panic. Why hadn't I stuck to birds? But he was still smiling, sort of. We both turned and squinted across the pasture, where the two bucks in velvet were making their way toward the shelter of the creek. "And the wildlife," I added. "Some mornings I see deer."

"Those are nice bucks," he said, sounding almost wistful. Then he straightened up again, and his smile broadened. "A bunch of us have been wonderin'. We come over the hill every morning and see this white car parked down here and think it's a cop!" He laughed, shook his head. "Well, sorry to bother you," he said, waving me back to my hillside. "We were just curious."

He pulled away, the crunch of his tires blending into the roar of morning traffic on the highway. I pressed the binoculars against my cheekbones again. The fox family hadn't paid a bit of attention to all this noise; they were too far away and too used to the highway, eastern Oregon's main north/south road. But it was all I could hear now, car after car of people heading for work. And I felt that look in the back of my head from each car, each pickup.

I've been getting that look for years. It's not that my neighbors are averse to watching animals from the side of the road—spotting scopes are nearly as common as TV remotes here. But people tend to be practical. If you're staring at something through a spotting scope, chances are it's because you have a use for whatever it is at the end of your vision. That deer will feed your family, that snag will keep them warm during the coming winter. Even that swarm of bees could put honey on the toast. So the man's puzzled expression and these imaginary stares that were making my scalp prickle—"a bunch of us"— felt all too familiar.

I got the same look from my own father the first time I went backpacking. Late summer, 1968. A rough year for us all. But Dad was 131 puzzled. How would strapping on a packsack and carrying a heavy load up to Buffalo Hump help me feel better? "Let me show you something," he said. He led the way through the garden and across the pasture to the log cabin where his old wooden pack frame hung from a nail beside his "tin pants" and a pair of caulk boots dangled by their brittle laces. "I had to pack in every week," he said. A week's supply of groceries, all the way up to the logging camps at Johnson's Mill, O-Mill, the Band Mill. It wasn't something he'd do again just for fun.

By the time my friend Betty Frances and I had reached our jumping-off point for the hike into the Hump country, we'd seen this look a lot. We'd felt it in the little store in Elk City where we had admired the huge diamondback skin stretched across the wall and bought a can of pork and beans for supper. And we'd seen it on the faces of the two men who'd stopped by our camp at the foot of the rock-and-rut road in their four-by-four pickups. They had taken one look at Betty's '61 Impala and understood immediately that we'd be going the rest of the way on foot. Like the storekeeper, what they didn't understand was why. "You're not gonna *fish?*" Of course the most puzzled look of all came from the game warden. By this time I had resolved to tell the next person who asked that yes, we were going after cutthroat, forgetting that Betty Frances had not only out-of-state plates but no fishing license.

The next summer, when we met to explore the Seven Devils, Idaho had seen at least a handful of backpackers, folks who trekked into the woods for no better reason than to be there. The ranger at the campground above Riggins wasn't any too happy about this development, though. A couple of weeks before, a group of hikers had left their packs behind—one of them had twisted an ankle or some damn thing—and expected him to lead a pack string back in there and retrieve them. "I have things to *do,*" he said. "You head back into that country, you get your own gear outa there." He looked skeptically at the gunnysack saddle bags I had tied on my dog. "How's the trail to Sheep Lake?" Betty Frances asked him. "You gotta be pretty husky," he said. There was a long pause while he looked us over, and then he said it again. "Pretty damn husky."

It's a compliment, I told Betty Frances. Now even she was giving me that look.

Of course, I reflected as the morning rush of traffic receded behind me, if I were just a little smoother about these things—if I could project that calm expertise I admire so much in people who can back fifth-wheel trailers into driveways while traffic builds up in the street behind them, for instance—I probably wouldn't attract more than a quick glance, no matter what unusual thing I appeared to be doing. But even now, three decades after those first backpacking trips, what people see is at the side of the highway is not a rancher checking the condition of her pasture or an artist capturing the morning light on the cottonwoods—just a woman gawking like a fascinated child. As a naturalist, an observer of stars and sego lilies and foxes, the feathered ones' paths through the air, I'm an amateur. In fact, it is the eagerness of a beginner's mind that pulls me up from sleep and out into the predawn dimness. Sometimes I've been dreaming: I've left Josh behind me somewhere in his baby stroller, or I'm opening the door of his bedroom again to find that open window. The irony of my own failures and empty places threatens to overwhelm me. But the earth is always here, just outside my door, under the wheels of my car, making a constant offer of relief, the sheer joy of listening for what it has to teach.

On the home place above the Clearwater, I glued pressed wild flowers into old Whitman Sampler boxes with carefully printed labels, but Mom knew the names of a only a dozen or so, the same ones I'd find between the pages of her old schoolbooks like ancient treasures. "No, there are no books about Idaho's natural history or the plants around this area," the librarian told us. Mom learned the birds listed in the encyclopedia, like the violet-green swallow, and taught us how to measure spring by the red-winged blackbirds' return in late February and the bluebirds' arrival in May. "People of the eaves, I wish you good morning, I wish you a thousand thanks," she said to the wrens. And we lay on our backs each August, watching the shooting stars and listening to the crickets promising fall. Dad, I thought, could do anything, period. But his knowledge of plants seemed to be limited to alfalfa and clover, how to get them grown and cut and into the barn before it rained, and that goddam Canada thistle and why-would-anyone-actually-*plant* morning glory. He argued, too, that no matter what my 4-H forestry leader said, bull pine and yellow pine were not just different stages of the same species, the ponderosa. "Norris is a good man but he's never been in the woods," Dad said. I knew what he meant: "went to the woods" carried the same kind of weight as "went into the service."

133

Now I have a shelf of bird books, star books, animal books. Books about trees. The librarian has to make special computer adjustments every time I show up at the desk with another armload, and I'm her biggest Interlibrary Loan customer. My mother, who is still my mentor in these matters, contributes to the National Wildlife Foundation and the Audubon Society as well as the Nature Conservatory and the Sierra Club. But like the student who fails the test even when she thinks she has studied, I keep getting distracted. How can I memorize genus and species when I open Ben Gadd's *Handbook of the Canadian Rockies* and find a picture captioned "a gray jay, thinking"? Or a passage like this one: "Some plant species, such as the beautiful calypso orchid that blooms around Jasper in May, must be fertilized by specific insects, in this case the golden northern bumblebee. It must be a queen bumblebee, for only the queens are alive this early in the spring; the workers and drones come later. Further, it must be a young, inexperienced bee, for the orchid manages to attract it and effect pollen exchange without providing any nectar. Wow!" Or this, further down the page: *"Everything you see around you is the product of 3.6 billion years of seasonal ecology. Everything is smarter than we think it is."*

And really, no matter how much I learn about the movements of stars and of orcas or how many birds I learn to recognize by their outlines against the sky, I know there is a deeper curriculum. I need to unlearn the illusion of separation. I need to unlearn "nature." I want to know what the Cayuse and Umatilla and Walla Walla People know. Not a series of intricately understood facts, though those can be all-important, but a relationship to reality. They would probably smile to hear me say this. It's not a secret.

So I rise early to find the curlews who will return to cry their long-billed circles over the desert every year on the anniversary of Josh's birth. Or to watch the summer's spotted fawns climb the riverbank every morning just after sunrise on their way back up the hill to the shelter of the trees. Or the lazuli buntings who land in a royal-blue surprise in our back yard every Mother's Day morning.

This summer I discovered the grace of mating osprey—the female rising from her clutch of eggs to welcome him circling back to her, his wings beating a balance for them both. The curve at the neck of the blue heron pushing through the air can take my breath away. So can the swallowed-fire colors of wood ducks. Sometimes what I see makes me smile: the shoulder-bumping of a robin and a magpie on the telephone wire; or the cliff swallow who settled down on the wire by the kestrel, staring in the opposite direction, then suddenly drove the kestrel over the ridge, a miniature mob of one. Or the coyote who stood at the edge of the freeway looking left and right, waiting for just the right break in the traffic to let him cross four lanes of asphalt and keep "going along." And the young fox who leaped to attention one morning—he'd been lying at the edge of the ravine road letting the magpies walk up to his belly as he watched a doe graze just across the gulch—and ran a few feet down the road, then stopped and sat down as if he thought he'd be invisible as long as he looked away. I watched the mating dance of mourning doves out my kitchen window, and one evening, a wild turkey dropping in for the leftover seeds (an emu! was my first thought). A sharp-shinned hawk wheeled past my ear to lift a goldfinch out of the air quicker than a gasp. A squirrel, sated with sunflower seeds from the feeder, took a nap on the maple limb just outside my kitchen window, his legs dangling over the branch like a sleeping child's.

Maybe what I'm doing is what Gadd calls "seasonal ecology," looking closely, noticing the ways in which everything depends on everything else. But I don't keep a bird list, and if you asked me to tell you what I know about the red fox, all I could do is point. So what can I tell my son? When I watch a trout rise in a dark pool of the rushing Lostine, or the line of red like a giant's petroglyph catching the first sunlight on the rock ridge above Ice Lake, or the quick sideways leap of the fox startled into flight, or hear the five-note call of the varied thrush and remember seeing one for the first time, his Thanksgiving colors lighting a November world, all I know is that whatever happens, happens inside my body. I move through the world differently on those mornings, as if I've been practicing T'ai Chi without moving.

There's something important right under our noses, I keep thinking. Maybe this is what I want Josh to see when he drives up into the Blue Mountains after work to look for cougars and elk and nesting great horned owls. There's something beneath the asphalt that we're

135

missing—and our missing it is costing us everything. It's not that I think we all need to become vegetarians or even fence off all streams compromised by flowing through lands where cattle graze, which was a bitterly contested ballot measure issue in Oregon not long ago. (The *No on* 38 signs are still up, out by the "Ler 'er Buck" sign on the freeway.) The truth is, when I'm sitting above the fox's pond waiting for the sunrise, I'm not thinking at all. It's as if I'm leaning back into the river instead of the weathered gatepost—letting the current hold me up. But on the way home, sometimes, or in my kitchen when I turn back to the sink or the stack of student papers waiting on the table, I know that what I'm after is a relationship to the world that would let us all heal. Could we begin again? Could a society built on racism and genocide—at least partly because of its concept of "nature"—change? What if we listened to the old stories from this continent, the stories that tell about our mutual obligations to each other, two-legged and four-legged and winged animals and plants, rock and water and wind? And about the gifts these beings are willing to give us, too. What if we smiled at the word "manage" as we smile now at these "primitive" ideas?

"I don't know, Mom ..." I imagine Josh teasing me, the way he sometimes tries to deflate my sputtering anger at the most recent headline, his eyes shining. But listen, Josh, I want to say. Every fall in my American Literature class I find William Bradford's description of the Pilgrims' first impression of North America: "What could they see," he asks, "but a hideous and desolate wilderness, full of wild beasts and wild men?" The more I think about it, the more I hear it all in those words. Slavery, Sand Creek. And Payoopayoo Maqsmaqs, the Walla Walla leader who signed the 1855 treaty but six months later was dead, mutilated, and skinned, just up the road from where we live now. Mr. Peabody's coal train. All of it. If "nature" is something other, something "out there" to be feared and subdued and reshaped in our own image, what else could have happened?

But I take comfort from that coyote at the edge of the freeway. I think he made it. I couldn't stop—like everyone else, I was on the freeway—but as long as I could see him in the rear view mirror he was still standing there, checking from left to right. I read recently that the coyote is the only animal whose numbers have actually increased since 1492. This despite a campaign against coyotes so sustained and so vigorous that a young neighbor of ours, who liked to skin coyotes in his kitchen, once tried to convince Dean to join him, charter a light plane and shoot coyotes from the air. The bounties would make us rich, he said. Government agents, more professional but every bit as dedicated, set out poisoned bait for years. But as the Cayuse and the Nez Perce and dozens of other Peoples could have told us (and did tell us), Coyote deals with adversity with an amazing if goofy resilience. Coyote's adversities, in fact, are why we're here at all, according to Nez Perce creation stories. Had he not slept through the naming ceremony and showed up late—if he'd had the intelligence of the fox or the courage of the grizzly or the massive power of the buffalo—maybe he wouldn't have been chosen to be Icyeeye, the transformer, preparing the way for human beings. Coyote was the right choice for the job, no question. Who is more like us? From time to time on his journey up the river Coyote gets himself in trouble with his curiosity or his appetites, and his friend Fox has to jump over him four times to restore him to life, but he rises up again and gets the job done. According to that *Smithsonian* article, officials in Los Angeles trap over five hundred coyotes in the city every year. They "destroy" them. That sounds like adversity to me. So I suppose it might even be good news, in the long run, for us all.

But in the short run, killing a coyote can carry a heavy price. There are stories to warn us about that, too. I remember the day Dean and Josh brought home a coyote skin—one of those father-son camping trips trying to fix things—and I knew, I knew. "Oh no, oh no," I said before I could stop myself.

"Don't worry, Mom. I won't shoot any more coyotes," he tells me now.

But of course people do. Not bad people, either. The ranchers and loggers and wheat ranchers here in eastern Oregon, all those people looking at the white car parked at the foot of the hill every morning, claim to have a better relationship to what their citified critics call the environment than the critics themselves. After all, they say, their bottom line is long-term survival rather than immediate profit, and many of them have protected watersheds and rotated pastures for years.

137

But they are singing the same song you might hear whistled on the pavements of Wall Street, if people there whistled. It's the vision of the Western world, the one that got my own family into so much trouble all those years ago. Life as Capital.

Even at school, learning is a product, we are told. We're competing for a market of student consumers. Some mornings when I pull into the college parking lot, I stay in my car, watching the fog lifting from the Umatilla and the morning gray-green foothills of the Blues. Then I close my eyes and go back to Ice Lake. I see the red rock ridges turning gold and watch the light coming down their curving slopes to the tips of the alpine firs out on the island. I follow that deadfall spruce down into the dark water. The light is far above me. Now I'm a brook trout rising toward that light, breaking the surface of the world. I see the mule deer weaving through the scrub willow, and then I am that deer, my summer coat red in the sunrise, dipping my dark nose into the water for a morning drink. Snow-cold, sweet. Above the circle of rock in the sun-filled air a falcon soars across the water toward the island fir. Wind pushes against the edges of my wings, ruffles the tips of my feathers.

When I open my eyes, I'm ready to go inside.

Each fall as I return to school I carry a new summer's visions with me. One July morning, parked by the side of the road, I watched two young foxes stand on their hind legs, and holding their mouths open but not biting, place their forepaws on each other's shoulders and dance a circle—once, twice, three times around. Another day, while I waited for sunrise on the ridge behind their den, a red fox came flowing across the meadow and trotted up the hill to within a few yards of where I was sitting: a gift of motion and sunlight. When she saw me she stopped, then came a few steps closer, lifting her slender chin above a fur so white it might be feathers.

It's all around me. All I have to do is look. But sometimes it catches me by surprise. Late in August, with summer almost over, I had stopped at the local Mini-Mart to buy ice and worms for an early morning fishing trip with Josh when one of the crew-cut men coming out with cups of steaming coffee waved his fruit pie at me. I didn't recognize

138

him at first. "I know where you're headed," he called across the asphalt. "You're going out to keep an eye on those foxes!" I grinned back at him—two kids with a happy secret.

It's a start, I thought. I could hardly wait to tell Josh.

# Roots

Tessie Williams was explaining the root feast ceremony to a roomful of college students and staff, her creased face bright with captured light. It takes a week of hard work to prepare the first roots, she told us. Girls and young women follow the elders, who show them where the roots live and how to press in the digging stick and then cover the small opening so that it doesn't leave a scar in the earth; and how to clean the roots, and peel them. You're supposed to stay with them, really, she said. At the longhouse. Finally, when everything's ready, there's the feast, served by the diggers and the male hunters. The three sacred roots, deer and elk and salmon, huckleberry and chokecherry. And *chuus*, water. After this thanksgiving feast, everyone is free to dig roots for their families for the coming year.

A woman in the audience raised her hand. "It sounds as if these ceremonies require time away from jobs, or from classes here at the college," she said. "What do you do when people don't understand these obligations?" I waited. This year's performance goal was to increase student diversity. Tessie smiled. "When it's time," her quiet voice said, "people say, 'The roots are dancing.' They want us to come get them, you see. They offered, all those years ago, to help the people. They're waiting for us." She paused, letting us all breathe silence. "Our young people will hear them when they are ready."

"But teachers should excuse Native students from classes," the woman told Tessie. She didn't know that we already do—like most administrators, she had never asked—but my sense of irony was diluted by something larger, an almost visual image of two people talking past each other, words flying over the other's shoulder and out into the emptiness. Two different concepts of time. It made me think of the raven I saw once at the North Rim of the Grand Canyon, how he had whispered past me and out into the canyon and disappeared, just vanished into the air. I felt my body swaying, still dizzy along this border. Then I heard Tessie's voice, soft and steadying as a grandmother's hand against my skin. She was laughing.

What is time? we ask each other in the Native Lit. classroom. Is it a string, Christmas lights strung on a cord winking in darkness? A current pulled by gravity, spinning the blades of turbines on its way to the sea? Or is it like a lake you've stepped into? Does it touch you on all sides at once, drops of past and future and the now inseparable?

I was born on a late April day in the season for digging. Maybe they were having the root feast that very day. "When's the root feast this year?" non-Indians often ask, but you can't mark your calendar and buy plane tickets a month in advance, although you're invited and welcome. The root feast happens when the roots are ready. It might have been a cold spring the year I was born.

This year Dean and I can share a piece of chocolate birthday cake and still get to the longhouse in time for the grand entry of the Root Feast Powwow. I see Annie in her white buckskin dress. At first I'm not sure it's her, she looks so different from her American Lit. class profile with her hair braided high like that. Then she smiles.

Circle dances, inter-tribals. Suddenly the drum enters my chest, pushing against my ribs like a hawk stretching and shaking its feathers. The feeling subsides, then comes again. We stand to honor the women elders. There are only two of them tonight, and one dances with her elbow supported by a younger woman. Her feet turn inward the way my mother's do since her hip surgeries. I remember a woman at Warm Springs on the morning after the all-night winter dance. She was laughing at herself about something. "Old as I am, I still feel like a child sometimes," she had told us. Now a man in a wheelchair—I recognize him, Thea's uncle—is speaking. "My grandson," he says. "Twenty months old. It's his first time dancing." The little boy is pushing out of his mother's grasp and onto the floor. "And he's *ready!*" laughs his grandfather. Voices of the Drum rise into song, and the little boy turns back to his mother, uncertain. Then a man dances forward and the boy joins him. The people come out on the longhouse floor to meet the little boy, bending to shake his small hand and joining in the growing line behind him. He looks up at each of them, totters a little, but keeps dancing, leading his people around the circle.

Seven years ago Mom was in this longhouse with me for a Mother's Day root feast. We had driven the blue truck out into the rolling hills

141

that dipped into canyons, the land wearing its May finery, deer rising up out of the new wheat and disappearing into the brushy draws. She was here to help me endure the second Mother's Day without my own child.

And just a few weeks ago, we had stood together on the bank of the Clearwater, listening to the river's high runoff current. "I'm so grateful," she said. "Not only did I live, but I'm able *to* live." She had just come through a bad bout of illness. We felt the March sun on our faces, and she showed me the first biscuitroot, blooming at my feet. *Cous.* "It's so good to know the days have turned and it will only get better," I said. I was thinking of seasons; the dangers of ice and dark afternoons. "I try not to be afraid," she had answered. "I try not to think ahead."

I watch the dancers celebrating this returning gift, the roots of spring.

Another season—late October—and this time it's my mother's birthday, her eighty-second. We are driving up a mountain grade to find her birthplace, the old Dobson place at the top of the Gilbert grade, only thirteen miles from the Idaho river drainage where she has lived most of her life. This trip has been a long time coming. Eighty years. It's hard to explain why she has never been back.

All I have are pieces of the stories I heard when they were part of the motion of my mother's hands kneading the bread dough or stirring the jelly kettle with the big wooden spoon or slicing potatoes for supper. "Mama and Daddy were living on the Dobson place when I was born," she had said. "Daddy was working for the Dobsons; they were twins, and Mama liked both of their wives. Pearl Dobson helped her when I was born, I was named for her—and for Aunt Irene, of course. She was a good friend to Mama." And then, always, something else: "I've always wanted to see the place."

Of course, it wasn't the "old" Dobson place then. We have directions to it for today's trip only by chance; the friend of a friend who lives nearby and remembers the farm by its family name. Someone she knows only as Mary has inherited the land, we have been told. The friend

142

isn't sure how often Mary is there, though. We go past the turnoff and have to pull in to a farmhouse to ask directions. A boy comes out to meet us, weaving barefoot between the big brown dog and the blue-eyed Australian shepherd on the wet grass. He knows exactly where the old Dobson place is. "If no one's home the gate will be locked," he says. We wave goodbye to the dogs, who bark us back down the driveway, heads high. My sister guides the car between the potholes.

It's prairie land, just at the edge of the canyon made by the Clearwater. Camas Prairie, Nez Perce Prairie—names that had lived in my parents' mouths like grownup secrets. From the ridge above our barn on summer afternoons I could just glimpse a thin rim of yellow, as far in the distance as I could see, way off across the canyons. Other worlds. Pines and firs mark the rim of the narrow grade we have just climbed, and beyond them are blue mountains, the Bitterroots. An earthful of nourishment if you knew how to listen. The prairie is wheat stubble now, rolling fields stretching to the other rim of mountains on the west. Pale yellow, gold. I remember the part of the story I liked best: "Daddy was sewing wheat sacks out in the field, and when they brought him the news that he had another daughter, he threw both arms up in the air and whooped, and the needle went flying up into the sky." This year the wheat harvest has been over for two months, the roar and grind of circling combines come and gone, wheat already spewed into grain elevators or loading down the barges on the Columbia. Jill and I used to hide in the cool granary, loosening the hand-sewn string on the dusty gunny sack and chewing the sweet kernels like nuts.

At first I don't see the cable gate. Just a narrow strip of twisted metal. It's locked. Jill thinks maybe we could drive our little car under it, explaining to anyone who might notice that we are here to see where our mother was born. I have a quick picture in my mind of Mom claiming her place on the earth, her smile calming the driver of any muddy four-by-four rig that might follow us up the hill to the farmhouse or materialize out of nowhere like the stuff of nightmares. But of course you can't drive under a cable gate. And it's a rough mud-rutted drive, a slick-footed slide down this slope and then up again, too far for Mom's sore hip and impossible for Jill, although she's still

143

on the near side of sixty, only the same short step ahead of me she has always been.

So we get out of the car and I take a picture of Mom looking toward the farmhouse. It's been remodeled in the past few years and it has a green metal roof, the kind country people long for. No fires, no leaks, a good roof over your head. Permanent. But it isn't the house Mom was born in. "We lived in a little house for the hired man," Mom says. Will my photograph start new generations of misunderstandings? There's an old shed behind the farmhouse, but it seems impossibly small. "Of course, it probably wasn't very big," Mom thinks aloud. The land slopes down beyond the green-roofed house so we can't see the farm itself, and she's not sure which brother lived in this house. Or maybe this house has been built sometime in the past eighty years; after all, her family left when she was two. "There's a picture of me propped on a blanket under some little trees," she says. "I might recognize those trees." We all keep looking, as if somehow we could see what is beyond the house on the downward slope of this land. "I was born with the umbilical cord wrapped around my neck, and Mama always blamed that on crawling under the fence when she went up to the main house to visit Mrs. Dobson. So the houses must have been fairly close together."

It begins to rain. A light rain, but it's cold, definitely a winter's-coming day at the end of the most beautiful October any of us can remember. We get back in the car. "We'll have to try again in the spring," Jill says. Mom doesn't answer. Cottonwoods are still yellow as we near the bottom of the grade and I can see spots of bright red across the river, chokecherry groves, I've learned from Mom. There's a blaze of sumac turning wine-dark, its branches visible through the thinned ribbing of leaves. Does the body have a root, I wonder? And do small threads of it remain in the earth in the place where you were born? "When your dad was on the county road crew, just before he retired, they worked on this road," she says now. "Up this far, it's still in Clearwater County. They were right here, he said, by the Dobson place. He saw the name on the mailbox. He said he'd bring me up here to see it, but we never made it."

144

Why didn't they go? As we pull out onto the highway by the river, I can't help picturing it, a Saturday free from shiftwork and stolen from the daylight-to-dark job of raising the kids and the garden, the cows and sheep and pigs and chickens, the fences and haying and sprinkling and ironing, the baking and canning and sewing. Half a day, less than half a day. But people were living there, children of the people her dad had worked for. Not strangers exactly, but still. It would have meant trying to explain that you needed something that wasn't really theirs to give, because you were born onto this earth, the daughter of a hired man who had lived here before they were born.

My mother saved all the letters I wrote to her when Josh was born and gave them back to me not long ago. She had written Dad a letter every day when I was a newborn, too. Maybe it was because he was stunned at being discharged from the Navy so soon—I was born the day Hitler died, and three weeks later, the war in Europe ending, the Navy had sent him home from boot camp—but when the letters finally caught up with him, he simply lifted the cookstove lid and tossed them in, unread. "Did you say anything?" I asked Mom once. "They were already gone," she said.

Yesterday I added the photograph to the small box with my own new-mother letters. How much of this story will Josh understand? Enough to hold him upright on the edge of that blue canyon, his feet feeling for roots? When we are ready, Tessie had said. Then I put the envelopes into the mailbox, copies for my sister and brothers, and for each of their children. "Irene on her eighty-second birthday," I wrote, "looking toward the Dobson place where she was born."

# Teaching and Learning

It is still common knowledge in the Northwest where I have spent my life. The Cayuse and Ni Mii Pu and Umatilla and Walla Walla and Yakama and Salish-Kootenai People—and many others—understand that there is a natural role for every age of our living. At first we are learners, then providers and protectors. A teacher, they say, is what each of us becomes as we grow older, passing along what our lives have taught us. "It takes a long time to learn how to be a human being," explains a sign in the Yakamas' Heritage Museum. "Only the elders are wise."

So how did the Yakamas feel, I wonder, when I showed up to teach their children at the age of twenty-two?

"Why did you come here?" my first students asked me. We shared a high-ceilinged classroom in an old brick building called White Swan High School. ENGLISH, read the sign above the door. "Where else could I have gone?" I said. They smiled. Then they repeated their question.

There was so much I didn't know. I was aware that in Indian country education had meant perpetuating the master narrative, and I would get a glimpse of how heavy-handed that teaching had been when the yellow buses took us all out to where the highway dead-ended at Fort Simcoe, six miles past town, for the annual school picnic. Together we looked in the door of the dirt-floored guardhouse cell where runaway or defiant or baffled children had been locked in darkness after the fort became an Indian school. The kids and I both knew that our high school was still intent on the same mission. "You are here," our principal had told the new faculty, "to make these Indians and Mexicans and the poor white kids of this valley into useful, productive members of society. Just pretend you're in the Peace Corps." But at least, I thought, an English teacher's classroom was where the stories lived. I believed in the power of stories. Stories were subversive. They could question that master narrative. Break it open. I would have to

146

work within the structure—it was where the kids were—but I would teach them to question that structure. Together, we would use stories to challenge the big story they heard there.

I was a kid myself, of course. It was 1967. Even then, though, I knew that teaching was a way of trying to pursue my own question. How can I live with integrity on stolen land? Growing up above the Clearwater where I could see through those carefully taught myths about civilization and savagery had left me stunned and wondering. How could I look out my kitchen window at whatever river basin I had settled in without imagining the way the Indian people of this place must feel, now, as they looked at this same landscape? Where could I walk? But the questions I had been asking since childhood didn't get any easier to answer in the circle of classroom faces.

A teaching lifetime later, with enough snow in my hair now that I could pass for an elder myself, I still don't really know the answer to my first students' question, or my own. In fact, teaching constantly reminds me of just how little wisdom I have to pass along.

On the last day of spring term, I sit knee to knee in my tiny office with Amy. She has come in to pick up her paper on "Kaddish"—which she wrote in Ginsberg's style, leaving me breathless—and to say goodbye. Amy thinks I know more about Ginsberg than I do. She's off to the honors college in Eugene, grateful for what she has learned from us, she says, in her two years at the community college. "What I know now," she tells me, "is how much I don't know."

For a moment it comes back to me, the rush in the chest as I too imagined all that lay ahead. What I didn't know at Amy's age was that in my fifties I would be dizzy with it: that the starfield of my ignorance would explode, galaxies playing leapfrog in a photograph from the Hubble telescope, looking further and further out every day. I have seventy-eight books checked out now, the librarian informs me, her face shoved into neutral. But it does no good; I forget old knowledge as fast as I read new truths, and they're all slippery, the old words and new—wriggling off the hook, back into dark water. I think of all the voices of America I haven't discovered yet, and all the things I don't quite understand about the ones I do recognize.

"Yes," I tell Amy now. "I understand. Sometimes—in the middle of a sentence—I think, 'How can I even be *teaching* this class?'"

"Oh, no," Amy says, genuinely startled. "You know *everything!*"

I look at Amy. How could I explain? Does she know that I still haven't read *Ulysses*? That I am baffled by the automatic debit machine at Albertsons? I don't know Spanish or Sahaptin or Greek, I can't always tell Mozart from Haydn. Until last year I thought micro-brew meant that microbes had been used in the brewing process, and the only thing I can do with my new office phone is pick it up when it rings and say hello. I've forgotten how to use sines and cosines, even tangents; I don't understand the CIA, the SAT's, the Gulf War, digital anything. I close my eyes and see canyons and mesas, but I don't know the names of the grasses that grow there, or the medicines they hold in their stems. I don't know the secrets of bears, or why people shoot magpies, or what will happen when they burn the nerve gas thirty miles up the road from my house. I don't know how to live with the stories of Sand Creek and Eureka and the Wallowa Valley and the Wada Tika Paiutes' December walk, barefoot and in leg irons, from Burns to Yakima. Was my mother's breast cancer caused by intentional releases of radiation from Hanford? How could Thomas Jefferson have written those words and not meant them? Can you be an alcoholic if you don't drink? I remember looking at the wine glass and thinking of my son, *do this in remembrance: this is his body, his red blood turning black*... to swallow and be swallowed by that blackness, is that what it's about? Lately I've begun to wonder about sanity, whether there's really any such thing.

What should I tell the mother who asked me what to do about her boy, who has started down the cracked and crystal highway? How do I make him turn around, come home, she wants to know. She misses him so much she knows she will die of it, choke on this grief too dry to swallow. I don't know how to answer the question Josh asked me when he was four: "Mom, is it dangerous to be a grownup?" I don't know how to forgive myself.

But I hug Amy—she lets me hug her—and I say, "Soar," and I promise to watch the skies, and she smiles and walks out into her life. I think about some words I heard the middle-aged writer and teacher Thomas King say, something a Blackfeet elder had asked him when he told her

148

what he did for a living: "You're pretty young to be telling stories, aren't you?" Then I lock my office door and walk out into the early summer evening.

Still, I've been a teacher for thirty-three years. Everyone has to earn a living, right? And I have tried to do it well. But I wonder if being a teacher is the way to live on stolen land. Would Joseph have approved? Or Toohoohoolzote?

Teachers have teaching-dreams. We've forgotten to go to class, or we realize we're standing in front of the room in our fraying sleep-shirt. Once my classroom was on fire. This time it's just a meeting, some kind of conference. "I don't tell lies to Indians," says the man—a teacher, introducing himself to the others. Say your name, and one thing about yourself. I am in this dream yet not in it, looking sideways at the man and at myself watching him. Sliding into my question.

Then I am awake, my throat burning. I close my eyes, but he is gone.

"How do you know?" I had wanted to ask him. "How can you be so sure?" I lie in the early morning light trying to catch my breath, as if I've been suddenly dropped from a place far above me.

In the community college—it's just over the Horse Heaven Hills and across the Columbia from my first teaching job—only a few of the students are Indians. There are also baseball players, mothers, out-of-work loggers and mill workers, recovering addicts. Some are Walmart clerks and some are just kids rooming together, taking turns boiling Top Ramen for dinner. Some people's hands have cut asparagus and tossed watermelon up into the waiting trucks, or bucked bales in the sun. I suppose the man in my dream was a reflection of my efforts to pursue truth. If you don't tell lies to Indians, my theory has been, you won't be telling lies to anyone else either. "It's all part of the same story," I say to all my students. "What happened to the Nez Perce and whatever happened to you last weekend." They look at me, amazed, puzzled, stunned, curious, bored.

I am not as sure of my strategy as I was in 1967. But if anything, I'm even more passionate. It's as if I'm always listening to a voice. Virginia

149

Woolf's "Angel in the House" whispered admonitions for submission and decorum, but this is a different kind of presence. She hangs around the classroom, arranging the desks in a circle. She waves her fist in the air, not her wings. She stabs me with her union button. She reminds me that I know, from the inside out, what it's like to be the child of those who wanted something—they thought it might be in the books—more than they wanted air. But they ran headlong into that beadle holding out his arms, no entrance to this library. Not enough money. Wrong clothes. Wrong gender. Or just wearing the wrong face.

"Tell the truth," she whispers. "It will be enough. And—help *them* tell the truth."

But I wish I could share the confidence of that man in my dream. Sometimes I feel as if I'm walking out over the rapids of our ongoing history on a rope as thin as grass stems. Maybe I'm just telling lies of my own. It's easy to do. Most of the harm that has been done in the classroom has been done with the best of intentions.

"Trust the stories people tell you," I tell students as the Native Lit. class begins. "If you read about Indians in a book, be skeptical." Yet I take news clippings in to share with them as if we can find truth in these printed accounts of our daily lives. "Listen to this," I said one early October day. "Did you think of our class when you heard this story?" This time it was a young gay man, beaten and burned and tied like a scarecrow to a wooden fence on a frozen Wyoming plain. We had just finished reading about Harley in Leslie Silko's novel *Ceremony*—Harley, who dies like Matthew Shepard, bleeding and tied to a fence on a cold fall night.

Sometimes, like that day, I just sit there with my hands full of newsprint. My students look at me, waiting, but I suddenly realize I don't know what to say.

150

Other days I do better. I have a theory, and the stories are teaching aids. See? For instance: a clipping from the *Confederated Umatilla Journal*, the monthly newspaper of the Cayuse/Walla Walla/Umatilla Peoples. It didn't make Pendleton's *East Oregonian*, although the photo is striking: a man named Liberty standing next to a three-foot-tall basalt rock which is poised, almost unbelievably, on one small protruding tip. He's an artist, this Liberty. All over the Reservation and up and down the east end—the rocky end—of the Columbia Gorge, he balances rocks. Environmental art. It's an amazing feeling to come upon one of his rocks, or a whole row of them, leading the eye down a sagebrush ridge and off into the Blues. Once, on my way to Portland, I saw one of his creations between me and the river, then another, half a mile down the road. Another. The earth-bone landscape between Boardman and Arlington was singing. And then, incredibly, a glimpse of someone kneeling on the dark gray outcropping above the highway. Liberty, balancing. It was like having an eagle swoop down over the car.

He's been in the *Journal* before. But this time the headline is different. "Gilliam County to Liberty: Cease and Desist."

"It's the two cultures' world-views," I said to my American Lit. students. "Two different attitudes toward the land. If nature is frightening, something to be distrusted in its "wild" state, something to be subdued and neatly trimmed—managed—then looking out your window and seeing a stranger up on the bluff picking up rocks is a clear signal. Call the police." They looked at me. "What would you do if you glanced out your window and saw a man in your back yard, making a rock stand on end? Or touching a flower, or picking up a feather?"

We had been reading Bradford and Cabeza de Vaca and Sayatasha's Night Chant. Their heads were swimming. Mine, too.

Sometimes I just put the clippings up on the bulletin board beside my office door. It isn't really my space, this bulletin board; my office is wedged in between Human Services and Anthropology. For months the only thing they had on the board was a poster urging foreign service. Before I knew it my clippings had spread like cheat grass across the brown cork, and people were stopping to read them.

151

But I didn't think anyone had plowed through the story about Belgian King Leopold's personal slave kingdom in the Congo. Should I highlight the key lines? I wondered sometimes as I rushed past, my arms full of books. The part about how all this happened less than a hundred years ago? How the shock waves are still killing people? Or maybe the part about the British shipping clerk who noticed—as if no one else had eyes—that though the ships came in loaded with ivory and rubber, they returned loaded with guns.

One winter, as I drove past the still-lighted Christmas trees across from Denny's in the January morning dark, I remembered the Indian storyteller who had visited our class. "Don't be afraid to feel joy," he told us. "To live." But after we let go of Whitman's buoyancy this term and set sail with the Realists, the reading assignments in American Lit. would be anything but cheerful. The Realists would shade into the Naturalists and biological determinism. It's the season of boarding schools, our consolation only Zitkala-Sa and John Milton Oskison and D'Arcy McNickle showing us that it was possible to cling to the wreckage and survive. And then, reaching for something to steady us, we would find the splinters and shards of "The Waste Land." So, I thought, what if I began each American Lit. class session by reading a poem that would make us feel happy? Maybe it was instinct, a balancing act of my own. Shoring fragments, T. S. Eliot might have called it.

I started confidently with Luci Tapahonso's poem about the visiting uncle drinking Hills Brothers coffee. Good to the last drop. The class was quiet; they didn't know how to take it. I looked out at their faces. Nobody's ever read them a happy poem, I thought. By the time we got to her poem about meeting George Strait in the airport, though, a couple of the women were laughing. I read Naomi Nye, Joy Harjo's circling eagle. Gary Gildner's Warsaw baseball poems. Fishing poems; and Robert Wrigley's love poems to his wife, Kim Barnes. "What the River Gives." "This is from my home town," I said. "The Clearwater— that stretch just below Lenore. Do you know that river? When I read this poem, I can smell the water."

They loved it. Even after the light came back and spring returned to our valley, we kept it up. We were into Viet Nam literature by this time. "Where's our happy poem?" the baseball player would ask on the days I forgot.

Then it was fall again, that mid-October day after the murder in Wyoming. Outside my window a white moon was waning. The chestnut tree below me was balancing its checkbook, half green, half rusted gold. Clouds so dark they were purple pushed against the foothills of the Blues, streaked with silver light across the valley where it was raining. The day before, in Native Lit., we had read Wendy Rose's poem about a mother at Wounded Knee. "Would have put her in my mouth like a snake / if I could, would've turned her / into a bush or a rock if there'd been magic enough ... not enough magic to stop the bullets, not enough magic to stop the scientists, not enough magic to stop the money." What does she mean? *She means that it will never stop.* The words had torn from Ruby's chest before she knew they were spoken. Her dark eyes were focused on something no one else could see. My hand reached out, but she was sitting on the other side of the circle. ("What do white student think when they hear these things?" she would ask me after class. "Does it change anything for them?")

The story I had cut from "The West" section of *The Oregonian* showed a picture of the rail fence where they tied Matthew Shepard to die. Next to this story was a smaller one about radioactive uranium tailings left on the banks of the Colorado River. The mining company wanted to "cap" them with earth. I left the stories together on the bulletin board. Would anyone think of *Ceremony*, Harley's body hanging on the barbed wire just outside the abandoned uranium shafts in the New Mexico darkness? As I had driven down the hill past Denny's that morning the radio promised anti-gay demonstrations at Matthew Shepard's funeral.

I thought about the tiny clipping that had been taped to my office door for so long it was starting to yellow, something Barry Lopez wrote once: "I believe, as much as I believe in the force of gravity, that all that stands between us and perdition—social disintegration, economic havoc, biological compromise, spiritual poverty—is the kind of discerning thought that helps us spot a lie, no matter how sophisticated or common-sensical those falsehoods might be." But I didn't know a poem that would balance Matthew and Harley and the Indian woman who had "expected my skin / and my blood to ripen / not be ripped from my bones / like fallen fruit ... peeled, tasted, discarded."    153

None of David Liberty's rocks stand forever, I know. A gust of wind, maybe just the changing moon, pulls them back to earth. Leslie Silko had said that you don't stop the Destroyers by fighting back—that just feeds the destruction. But the Destroyers' plans won't work if someone is watching. Witnessing, paying constant attention. Another kind of balancing act, maybe, teetering upright in the brief time we have between daylight and dark.

"It takes a while," Tom tells us. "The Chinese say it takes five lifetimes." At the early morning T'ai Chi class, our teacher is the youngest person in the room. I smile, trying hard to learn patience. Outside, it's snowing. "Practice in the snow," Tom says. "It will show you where your feet are going."

I have learned more about teaching from this young man—an anthropologist working for the Confederated Tribes to help clean up Hanford—than from any other teacher. He is infinitely patient, respectful, insightful. He knows how to see and when to point out what he sees, when to let us discover it ourselves. He laughs easily. He loves what he's teaching. But even his generous spirit cannot quite stifle my impatience. Why is my brain so thick? Why does it take me a month to learn a simple sequence of movements that last only a few seconds?

"Bette, you're thinking too much," he tells me. "Smile." He knows my secret. "I know, I know. But I can't tell you how happy it makes me," I say. He nods.

I am hungry, I am a greedy learner. "Got time to do it again?" he asks. Yes, yes. Again, and again. (I can park down by the science building, go straight to my classroom ...)

Once, in high school, I wrote a petition and got thirty girls to sign it. We all wanted to take wood shop. No. No girls. We couldn't take Ag., either. There would be talk about breeding.

"Next week, we'll start Chen Style," Tom says. "And then, would 154 you all like to learn a sword form?" My heart leaps. Five lifetimes. Carry Tiger to the Mountain, Stork Cools Wings. Swallow Flies Through the Forest and "Captures" the Moon. Slowly, slowly.

It's easy to be patient with my students. When we talk and read and write about racism, for instance, or homophobia, or sexism—and especially about the subject they all know first hand but keep wrapped in silence, the limitations based on social class—I understand how painful this learning can be. Each student teaches me something. Stories I have never heard, things I have never thought of. But it's difficult to be patient with myself when we talk about Indians. "*Must* we talk about Indians?" someone once asked me. "I signed up for American Lit. Shouldn't we start with the Puritans?" How can I show them how to see what our culture teaches them not to see? Watching PBS one night, I heard the announcer say, "The Mormons settled at Great Salt Lake because this was land nobody else wanted." How do my Indian students hear words like these, I wondered, casual phrases in which their existence has simply been erased? Can I even begin to help all my students recognize this cultural amnesia?

Overt hostility is easier. We share stories in writing class, so everyone hears how a mother hurried her kids out of the city pool when Michael's Indian Recreation bus arrived, or Kari's father warned her to stay away from the reservation. Clerks in Walmart send out their Code Blue announcements every time Charlotte's family walks through the automatic door. Richard tells us how he was stopped at the door of the antique shop. "We probably don't have anything you might be looking for." A carload of young men pinned Brad's pickup in the Mini-Mart parking lot, bumper to bumper; another yelled taunts at Willa as she walked home from Safeway. Students feel terrible when they hear these stories.

But between the casual and the brutal are the trappings of everyday life. The caricatures of Indians that decorate the gym floors and hats and jackets; John Wayne and Kevin Costner and the highway signs that say "Now leaving the Umatilla Indian Reservation." And it's in between that most of my students live, most of the time.

"There aren't any real Indians left, anyway," some of them say.　　155

But some of them catch a glimpse of it, this huge shadow, and they ask me, *What now?*

"I may not come back in the fall." It was a young Indian mother, a student who had become a friend. She sat in my office, almost whispering. Then she paused, looking past my head at the skyline outside the window. "This is the first time I've said it aloud."

"I remember this one day in high school," she said after a moment. "We sat on one side, the Indians and the Hispanic kids, and the wheat rancher kids sat on the other side. Nobody made us, we just did. The teacher was sitting on his desk, I remember, talking to a wheat rancher's daughter. 'I can draw a line right down this room,' he said. 'The people on this side will go to college and have good lives. The people on this side will drop out and live on welfare.'"

I watched her face.

"We were just stunned," she said. "Nobody said a word. Because he was *right*. And I remember thinking, 'You can go to *college?*'"

She looked directly at me. "I'm tired of people watching me fail," she said.

"Lucy, getting a C in math isn't failing," I had already told her. Even though I knew what she meant, and she knew that I knew. I thought of what she had said once in class. "Every day I dread driving into town." I had waited while the other students weighed her words, imagining their weight. No one shifted in a desk, no paper shuffled. Then a door shut somewhere down the hallway and we all began breathing again.

I remembered so many stories. Like Lucy's friend James, that paper he wouldn't let his writing group see. Happy to meet his old friend on the first day of school—a boy who had gone to live with his father for a year but was back for seventh grade—James had smiled. The friend said, "Wagon burner!" The boy's new friends had laughed. Or Lucy herself, with the manager's hand on her wrist, dragging her back through the lunch crowd of high school students to the counter where the clerk would say yes, she had paid for her Nachos. Or Lucy just last winter—she had walked out of her evening class an hour before the discussion on 'justice' would be over—sliding deeper into the hot bath. "Mom," her little girl had told her, "you should have stayed."

156

And Starla. "At first, I thought the poem was talking about people," she had said in class that day. "But then the narrator says, 'I feared I was beginning to understand his language, which was not human,' so I realized the poem must be about wolves." That search for the words to say, no, Starla. It's about Indians.

I wasn't sure what to say to Lucy, either. Is watching enough? What is it that I am witnessing? I felt myself slipping. Some days, I am not sure that there are enough stories to balance the pain, for Indian students, of simply coming to class.

Snow again, coming down hard. I'm sitting in the Les Schwab Tire Center in my home town waiting for Mom's new snow tires to be mounted. The man in the down jacket next to me is talking just a little too loudly. "It's crazy," he says. "Plumb crazy. Next thing you know they'll be tryin' to take over the courthouse."

His friend pushes back in the orange plastic chair. "Long as they can still pick up their welfare checks," he says. He grins. I look out the window toward the river and the dark trees on the other side.

"I don't understand it." It's the man's wife. Her glasses are still steamed with condensation. "I thought we won the war, years ago. People came here and built this country. Bridges, roads ... I thought we'd civilized this place."

"There you go," says the friend. They are sharing the bag of popcorn Les Schwab offers as you come in the door, its salty promise mingling with the smell of new rubber and wet boots. Behind us, an Indian man in a red Pendleton blanket jacket and a black cowboy hat is making arrangements for his tires. I stand up. But he is turning toward the door. On his way out, he nods to the others. "Mornin', Andy," one of them says.

I've been following the stories in the *Lewiston Morning Tribune*, so I know what this is about. It's about sovereignty. The U.S. Ninth Circuit Court of Appeals has just decided that the Nez Perce Tribe has jurisdiction over non-Indians living on purchased land within its 1863 reservation borders. Feelings are running high. And if the lower Snake River dams aren't breached, are the 1855 treaty rights to salmon and steelhead abrogated? And then what?

The rights of Indian people to self-determination have been making hard talk all across the country. The most chilling was something I heard during the first Makah whale hunt. "I am anxious to know where I may apply for a license to kill Indians," wrote a man who lives in

California. "My forefathers helped settle the West and it was their tradition to kill every Redskin they saw. 'The only good Indian is a dead Indian,' they believed. I also want to keep faith with my ancestors."

What now? What shall I tell my students? "Snow is helpful," I could say. "You'll warm up if you keep moving. Go outside, and see where your feet have been."

But how do we escape the bloody tracks of our history? I thought a lot about history and sovereignty during the week the college gives us between winter and spring terms, when I joined a local tour group for a trip to Ireland. The minute the plane touched down in Dublin I knew I was home. Of course, I wasn't, really. My father's grandfather, Augustus Lynch, had emigrated from Ireland. That's all we know. Nobody knows where he was born, or what part of Ireland he came from. He may have been Northern Irish loyalist, for all we know. We know there are some other Celtic great-grandparents, Highland Scots and people from Wales. As tribal ties go, of course, this is pretty thin stuff. Yet here I was, wandering around the St. Patrick's weekend street fair with everyone I saw looking like a cousin, somebody I should be kissing at a family reunion. When the tour bus left Dublin the feeling got even stronger. At Newgrange, the passage grave older than the pyramids, I saw the same spiral carving in the curbstones and in the womblike inner passage that I had seen in Arizona and New Mexico. We stood in total darkness and then an electric winter solstice sunrise reached in and touched us, leaving us changed. Above me the cathedral-like ceiling rose, rocks corbeled in and rain channels carved outside; rainproof, in Ireland, for five millennia. Why didn't we learn about this place in elementary school? people wanted to know.

158     In the interpretive center I saw pictures of Irish people living like Indians: the same tools, the same clothing, the same respect for the spirits in the river. The Celts were wanderers, our guide told us, traveling west to the sea, then back to the east every year. At night I ate the same salmon they had journeyed to welcome, all those years ago.

Of course, I already knew there were parallels between the Irish and the Indians. When I had read about the Indian Agent telling the starving Minnesota Sioux just before the 1862 uprising that if they were hungry, they could eat grass, I thought of the Irish bodies lying beside the road banks, their bellies bloated, their mouths stained green. Ireland used to be densely forested, but Queen Elizabeth I ordered the trees cut because they sheltered the Irish rebels, and of course she needed masts and wood for the fleet that would seize the spoils of the Americas from the Spanish ships and create the empire where the sun never sets. Felled Irish trees sent out to serve a dream of empire: it had a familiar ring. I knew the languages and religions of both peoples had been outlawed, and both the Irish and the Indians had been pushed into their own version of The Barrens where the conquerors hoped they would starve. Even the stories were similar—the little people, the death wail of the Banshee—and the music, the flute and the bodhran. And the dancing, the way it keeps both peoples alive, even today.

But I didn't know, as the bus traveled along, that I would want to bury myself in every roll of pastureland, every peat bog. It was an almost visceral feeling, this yearning, as if I could wrap the land around me and remember its texture and smell like a mother's old coat. I thought I knew the story of the rock-walled corners of Connemara where people tried so hard to grow enough potatoes to feed their children, but at first I mistook these for animal pens; some of them were just big enough for a cow to turn around in. When the driver explained what they were, my eyes filled with quick tears. Waitresses came around with their bowls of boiled potatoes, offering to add some to whatever was on my plate, usually including at least two other varieties, and I always said yes. At Navan Fort, where Emain Macha ran the race around the ditch with Conor's horses and Cu Chulaian grew strong enough to battle the hound of Ulster, I got locked in the museum, trying to slip back while the others were eating lunch for one last look at the replica of the hound's skull, and the skull of the Barbary Ape, the silver brooches and long brass horns. Maybe I just wasn't through yet, I told myself when it was so hard to get back on

159

the plane at Shannon Airport. After all, I was returning to the mountains and rivers of the Inland Northwest. To my family.

As friendly as the Irish were, I knew they were friendly because we were Americans, not because they recognized their cousins returned at last. Just who was I, even in Ireland? The Lynch name is a popular one. One kind of Lynches descend from the Celts; Lynch means fisher in Gaelic. Another kind, the ones whose name is common in Galway, were one of the fourteen "tribes" of Anglo-Normans sent to rule the land and fight off the fierce O'Flaughertys who held out in the rocks of Connemara like Modoc Captain Jack in his barren lava stronghold at Tule Lake on Oregon's southwestern border, fighting fiercely for these last stony homes. I stood in the dusk and looked up at the window from which James Fitzsimmons Lynch had hanged his own son, enforcing the Anglo-Norman code when no one else would do it, when everyone else supported his wife's Breton code of compensation for a life taken. "I hope I am not a great-granddaughter of this man, Jim," I told our driver as I climbed the steps of the tour bus. "It can't be helped," he said.

Back in my classroom, I kept the music in my head for weeks, and that feeling, too, of walking on the spring earth. But it's the stories that stayed with me. The way every curve of the narrow road, its banks white with blooming thorn brush in March, the way every river carries an old message. "So much suffering," Jim said as we crossed the River Boyne to leave Drogheda. "Three thousand people died, on both sides, when Cromwell came (*Stone dead hath no fellow,* another familiar echo). That round tower was the Loyalist stronghold, and here was where the Irish made their stand." I remembered the Cayuse, half of their two-thousand-strong community gone in one winter. How many people in my town knew that number? Here, it was in the stone, in the weathered wooden bridges, in Jim's voice. "Our people didn't need writing," an Indian student's grandfather had told her:. "We knew how to read the rocks." As we descended into Armagh, two dark helicopters flew across the sky, and Jim pointed to the hill above us where the Royal Ulster Constabulary was watching everything. Don't take pictures of anyone in uniform, he said, or look too long at the graffiti (UVF—CHILD KILLERS, in red paint on the pale yellow wall of the

160

low-income housing). The police station pushed its army-green walls against the sidewalk, and razor wire flew in wild circles above our heads. Across the street was the new prison, and a few feet away, the old, with broken window glass holding its own sharp vigil when I looked up from the bus window. Jim said everyone on both sides wanted a compromise, everyone except the extremists, and I remembered the Belfast mothers who had knocked on all those doors and begged for peace so their children could live. But I understood in my bones why the heart races and blood spills over something that happened in 1690. Linear time may be a concept invented by conquest.

I got home just in time for a week-long war. It wasn't real, the newspapers assured us. Just a practice war, hosted by the National Guard. Bombers flew low in formation, and fleets of transport helicopter shook the budding maples in our back yard.

Where can I walk? Along the Umatilla, I could smell cottonwood and willow and the sun on river rock. Above the pond meadowlarks told their stories, and the fox kits poked their noses up to see what it was all about. Blackbirds swung on last year's cattails making red and yellow promises. When I drove down the Columbia, I thought of the stories from Northwest Lit. class: salmon and those sisters, the wolf brothers and whirlpools and giants and children, Coyote and fire. The stories had taught me how the land was shaped, how things came to be on this land. They told me how to survive here. How to have hope, find courage when I'm afraid, seek balance, be wary of my human greed. They told me about the numinous. And almost, but not quite, they told me who I was.

I read somewhere that parts of Ireland and Scotland were once part of the Appalachians. This was a long time ago, the writer said, back when the continents were all one. Pangaea. All-earth. So we were home once, then, I couldn't help thinking. All of us.    161

Last year, in my final weeks of teaching, an Indian student called me Teacher. My mouth opened to deny it. *No, I am not that kind of teacher.* All I had done was urge him to tell his stories, watching from the back of the room as his listeners leaned, stunned, into his words. But he was smiling. He dipped his head slightly—a quick nod. Yes. He had already pointed out the picture of his grandmother from White Swan in the book on Northwest Indian basketry, and suddenly I was back in that first classroom at the foot of the sacred mountain thinking about stories and their secret power. It had not been mine to give, and it was not mine to give now. But it is there, I thought, waiting for us to discover it together.

# Seedlings

On the home place, ponderosa pines are returning to the cleared fields. I was in my teens when my father worried about the seedling pines that had sprung up in our neighbor's sloping pasture. "You need to get those out of there now, Jake, before they get any bigger," he said. "I want them," Jake grinned. "That's my forest." He had no livestock; his little corner of land was only a few acres, a place to live out of town. The trees are forty years old now. Whitetail disappear into them in the evening light, fading out again to check on their fawns who are running wild circles to the pond and back. I look at the seedlings growing on our own hill, scattering their way across the pasture in front of the cabin, climbing the slope behind the barn, and try to imagine how it was before my grandparents began cutting the big yellow pines.

For Dad, making this ranch had been a lifetime's work. Two lifetimes, really—his father's and his own. Stump ranching, he called it even after he'd dynamited the last stumps. But he said he was never going to cut the big bull pines up on the ridge above us, or the tall firs that lined the lane from the barnyard to the field or the trees in the corner of land below the east field, what we called "down in the woods."

Taking a walk into the lower woods, I remember the agony of that first logging, and how Dad worried over the angles of the skid trails and made sure there were no gashes on the trees left standing. Selective logging, just enough to help make the first payment on the land. Was that the winter that we had no meat? But there was no talk of sacrificing a few more trees to pay for new coats or medicines. Now it's been logged four times. Bugs, Dad finally said. Have to get those trees before they're bug-killed. Last spring's logging, fifteen truckloads, happened because of a heavy snow and thaw and windstorm that broke dozens of trees. The logger has left most of the slash lying on the skid trail. He says it's a new method of controlling the beetles. I can see a green metal roof through the scattered narrow tree trunks left standing.

Neighbors push right up against the southern fence line now, each house claiming its five acres. Some of them are vacation homes; the people in that green-roofed house, the one just below this tinder-dry slash, started a fire last summer by leaving a hot burning barrel after a weekend visit. I kick a dead branch with my shoe, wondering if my sister can move quickly enough to get out in time if this stuff ignites.

But I can't think this way, or let myself look too long at the skyline on the hill above the house, either, where the river of wind used to flow through the huge pines. There are enough trees on the hill to hold the soil in place, but I can see sky through their branches at the top of the ridge. It's funny, I thought the hill was higher. It seemed to go up forever.

Sunrise still sends those long silver fir-shadows across the east field all the way to the draw, though, and the speckled patterns of July clouds race to disappear behind the ridge above us. I watch the afternoon sun dipping below the ridge, leaning north in its summer journey almost as far as the tallest bull pine and bathing the place in the blue-green haze of backlit pine needles. The tangle of comfrey along the edges of the driveway is the same, and blackberries are turning red below the county road.

There are even more animals than when I was growing up. The flickers have come back, and there are bright towhees at the feeder, and black-headed and evening grosbeaks, Cassin's finches. A pair of red-tailed hawks are regular nesters, and last summer a peregrine falcon challenged them for hunting perches. Herds of elk move past the apple trees and cross the clearing on the ridge above us, and the reintroduced wild turkeys lead their chicks through the tall grasses. There were always deer, but not so many, so close: at least four whitetail does are raising their fawns in what's left of the lower woods, and they drift by 164 the living room window mornings and evenings. Sometimes, when we're sitting quietly, they come into the yard with us. At dusk we watch the fawns chasing each other in ever-widening circles, urging their mothers and the yearlings to join in too until the pasture where our big garden used to be is a maze of bobbing white tails, like a time lapse photograph of moving headlights in the growing darkness. We don't see cougars or bobcats as often as we used to, but one fall day Jill called me, amazed, to say she had just watched a young moose heading down to the pond.

One explanation for the wildlife recovery here is the absence of DDT. Bald eagles have returned to share the Clearwater's steelhead run, and great blue heron are common along the river now. Osprey build their nests at the tops of the biggest pines and circle above the current. But another reason is the loss of habitat nearby. What used to be a steep rocky hillside for poor people to cling to, trying to raise their families on land that wouldn't quite support them, is now prime real estate. The deep reservoir behind the dam on the North Fork has turned Orofino into a tourist town and Clearwater County into a place people come to retire. When my mother was trying to stop a potential dump site on land near ours, she discovered that a thousand people lived within a mile of it. Crawling through barbed wire fences was such a natural part of my childhood that the adjacent lands seemed part of the home place to me. But the woods below our fence line and beyond the east field, where we picked dewberries in the grass-covered wagon ruts and rode the horses through the old corduroy roads, are gone. Our place—only eighty acres plus the slope of hill above Jake's house, but much larger than the subdivided home sites around us— has become an unofficial wildlife refuge.

It's a strange roll of the wheel, one I still can't get used to. If we had to buy it, or buy each other out, the children in my generation could not afford the home place. Country living on acreage of this scale is for people wealthier than we are.

My sister lives here now, in the drafty old house on the "lower forty," the place we think of as home. Most of the upper forty above the benchland is inaccessible. Mom has agonized over a fair way to leave this land to all her children. There will be more logging eventually, I know, although the logger tells us that for some reason the pines on top haven't re-seeded. They should have, but they haven't. We might want to plant by hand, he says, if we want to assure a harvest for our children. I close my eyes. I see that skyline in my dreams, and I want Josh to see it again too, and Destiny, and Aaron and Angela and Jacob. And the new baby, Jared. Maybe they'll live long enough to hear the current of Chinook wind through the heavy branches of old trees. But

165

what fills my mind is another vision. Skid trails and splintered stumps, the smell of raw pine and diesel and the sound of falling yellow pines, that dead-weight crash.

Last spring, when the runoff creek above the house roared like a much larger river through the March air, I climbed and crawled through the brush to take a picture of the place where it enters the earth. I wanted to try to capture that mystery that my sister and I used to wonder over each spring: the miracle of its disappearance and its emergence below the barn at the head of the draw. The photograph wasn't as good as being there herself, but Jill was grateful. "I haven't seen it for so long," she said. The ranch, she says, is one of the few places, buffered from diesel fumes and herbicidal sprays, where she can still live. A strange and disabling illness has left her moving slowly and in pain I can only imagine, each step powered by sheer determination. Was it caused by radiation released from Hanford, I sometimes wonder? We're downwinders; we were little kids drinking milk from the family cow during the Green Run. Could it have been atomic testing in Nevada and Utah floating our way on the pink snow? She worries about all the things she can't do to take care of the place. Those trees that are filling the fields, she says—maybe we should talk to the people who could come in with big machines and uproot the trees for high-paying customers, the folks building malls and such. I don't say anything. I can't help hoping she likes the seedlings, too. The way they show the shape of the wind scattering its blessings and the places where water stays longest in the earth. In the late afternoon light, now, the field seems to glow.

"If those seedlings get much taller we won't be able to see the cabin," Jill said one morning as I sat at her kitchen table. I hadn't thought of that. The cabin our father had built when he was still a teenager was his way of claiming a man's place on the earth across the pasture from his parent's bigger log house. Jill had lived there as a baby; it's where I was conceived. We still measure spring by the first Easter lilies on the forest floor behind its walls, and the evening shadows around the cabin have always promised supper and rest, a yearning for peace. It will stand a while longer—it's well-built; hell for stout, Dad would have said—and he and my brothers re-roofed it years ago with leftover shingles his own father had split for the barn. John, who has been sober and healthy for a long time now, talks about doing it again. He wants to make sure it lasts. But sitting at my sister's kitchen table that morning, I imagined the cabin hidden, invisible, huddled between the tall firs at its back and the new young pines in its lap. Not many people would know it was there, and even fewer would know that a Ni Mii Pu tepee circle once marked the earth in that spot.

I suppose wanting the seedlings to take over the place again is silly, a romantic dream. Where do we belong if not here? Story after story tells of Indian people who were willing to share the earth with us, I remind myself on days when every step I take feels as if it's crushing something. It's a matter of finding a way back to that beginning place, five hundred years too late, and learning to begin again. What matters, I know, is what we do now. But what prayer can I sing? What ghosts will dance with me?

Last August I looked up in the sky and saw them. I had gone outside in the hours before dawn to check on the annual meteor shower, and there above me were the first northern lights I'd seen since I was a child. A green glow rose up behind the ridge above the east field, and clouds of light whirled across the sky. Pinkish mist, each wave racing toward the one ahead of it. It was a dance so fast my eye could not follow. A meteor streaked behind the light-clouds, then another, and another, and as the moon rose to join us the sky dancers gathered in columns of white light that stretched across the sky like human fingers reaching toward the earth. Lying on my back under all that swirling mystery, I felt myself sailing far out into the light-filled darkness. But the earth was holding me even then, when like a dizzy child I spun back into her lap. There were old stories in the ground beneath my shoulders. So much love, and so much pain. Tears and songs and footsteps, a look back over someone's shoulder; words that still hang like swarming bees in the most silent places. I lay in the cool darkness, listening. I could feel the presence of my family and all those people before us. How many eyes were lifted with mine to these August skies?

Just beyond the swift river of light swam the bright stars of the big dipper, the hunter, the bear. It was like looking into the Clearwater. The red and black rocks on the bottom are so close it seems you can

167

stretch your arm into that snowmelt current and touch them, but they're beyond your reach. The first time I saw the bear in the night sky was after our family's log house had burned and left us alone in the snow, and we had moved across the field into that little board shack beneath the ponderosa. It was the place where I had first understood that the Old Ones were with us, just beyond the limits of my vision. And it was there that my mother began teaching me what it means to be human. *Say thank you*, she told me. *Say you're sorry*.

Another meteor blazed behind the swirling light. I am still a child on this land, I thought: whispering only what I remember, simple words.